Praise for *The Dyslexia Checklist*

"The authors have (and current list of resources for parents, with the prevention and remediation of dyslexia. This is a valuable and unique contribution to the field."

> —*Louisa C. Moats*, EdD, nationally known authority on literacy and author of *Speech to Print: Language Essentials for Teachers*

"Comprehensive and accessible. . . . *The Dyslexia Checklist* presents a clear delineation of areas that must be addressed in literacy instruction. Each section describes the literacy component, provides useful background information—including a solid research base for each component—and lists helpful activities that can be used to teach skills and strategies to introduce lessons and strengthen learning. Classroom teachers, learning specialists, administrators, and parents will find this straightforward guide indispensable as a resource compendium and as a professional development tool."

> —*Esther Klein Friedman*, PhD, director, Academic Intervention Services, New York City Department of Education

"Contains the hottest topics and information for understanding, supporting, and teaching children with dyslexia. The authors' knowledge, practical focus, and down-to-earth strategies make this book an essential read for educators and parents."

> —*William N. Bender*, PhD, coauthor, *Reading Strategies for Elementary Students with Learning Difficulties*, 2nd edition and *Response to Intervention: A Practical Guide for Every Teacher*

"Offers educators and parents a comprehensive overview of the skills a dyslexic needs for success, plus effective strategies and techniques to empower students."

> —*Jone Bycel*, MS, BCET, board-certified educational therapist

Jossey-Bass Teacher

Jossey-Bass Teacher provides educators and parents with practical knowledge and tools to create a positive and lifelong impact on student learning. We offer classroom-tested and research-based teaching resources for a variety of grade levels and subject areas. Whether you are a parent, teacher, or another professional working with children in grades K–12, we want to help you make every learning experience successful.

From ready-to-use learning activities to the latest teaching framework, our value-packed books provide insightful, practical, and comprehensive materials on the topics that matter most. We hope to become your trusted source for the best ideas from the most experienced and respected experts in the field.

The Dyslexia Checklist

A Practical Reference for Parents and Teachers

Sandra F. Rief

Judith M. Stern

JOSSEY-BASS
A Wiley Imprint
www.josseybass.com

Published by Jossey-Bass
A Wiley Imprint
989 Market Street, San Francisco, CA 94103–1741—www.josseybass.com

Library of Congress Cataloging-in-Publication Data
Rief, Sandra F.
    The dyslexia checklist: a practical reference for parents and teachers / Sandra F. Rief, Judith M. Stern.—1st ed.
        p.   cm.
    Includes bibliographical references and index.
        ISBN 978-0-470-42981-5 (pbk.)
        1. Dyslexic children—Education—United States.   2. Learning disabled children—Education—United States.   3. Dyslexic children—Education—United States—Case studies.   I. Stern, Judith M. II. Title.
    LC4709.R44 2010
    371.91'44—dc22

                                                                    2009020131

Printed in the United States of America
FIRST EDITION
PB Printing   10 9 8 7 6 5 4 3 2

Contents

To the students who have motivated us, the colleagues who have shared with us, and the parents who have inspired us

Acknowledgments

We wish to thank

- Our loving and supportive families:
  - Itzik, Ariel, Jackie, Jason, Maya, Gil, Sharon, and Daniella (Sandra's)
  - Uzi, Talia, Naomi, and Emma (Judith's)
- Margie McAneny, our editor at Jossey-Bass
- The researchers in the field of dyslexia who continue to advance our knowledge about reading disabilities, how children learn, and how we can best teach them

About The Authors

Sandra F. Rief, M.A., is an internationally known speaker, teacher trainer, educational consultant, and author on effective strategies and interventions for helping students with learning disabilities and ADHD. Sandra is a popular presenter of keynote addresses, workshops, and seminars for teachers, parents, and other professionals throughout the United States and internationally. Previously an award-winning special educator (California Resource Specialist of the Year) with more than twenty-three years of teaching experience in public schools, Sandra is the author of several highly regarded books, including *How to Reach and Teach Children with ADD/ADHD* (2nd ed.), *The ADD/ADHD Checklist* (2nd ed.), and *How to Reach and Teach All Children in the Inclusive Classroom* (2nd ed. coauthored with Julie Heimburge). Sandra has also developed and presented several acclaimed educational DVDs, including *ADHD and LD: Powerful Teaching Strategies and Accommodations* (with RTI); *How to Help Your Child Succeed in School: Strategies and Guidance for Parents of Children with ADHD and/or Learning Disabilities;* and *Successful Classrooms: Effective Teaching Strategies for Raising Achievement in Reading and Writing* (with Linda Fisher and Nancy Fetzer). For more information, visit her Web site at www.sandrarief.com.

Judith M. Stern, M.A., is a teacher and educational consultant in Rockville, Maryland. She works with children who have learning and attention problems, as well as their parents and teachers. She is an experienced learning disabilities specialist, reading specialist, and classroom teacher. She consults with parents and schools and speaks nationally on learning problems, attention deficit disorder, and children's study skills. She conducts workshops for parents, educators, and mental health professionals. She is coauthor of four children's books on ADHD and LD, including the best-selling *Putting on the Brakes: Understanding and Taking Control of Your ADD or ADHD* (2nd ed.), and *Many Ways to Learn: Young People's Guide to Learning Disabilities*. More information is available at www.Judith SternEducationalConsultant.com.

Introduction

We have each been in the field of teaching students with learning disabilities for more than thirty years. During this time, we have worked with students in a variety of school settings and have been privileged to teach students at a wide range of grade levels, with and without special learning needs. Our own teaching experiences, training, and work with many gifted, dedicated colleagues have taught us much about helping students with reading difficulties. Along with other educators, we continue to seek new information about developments in the field and to strengthen our skill and understanding of how to best help children with reading disabilities. As good teachers know, there is always new research to consider and there are always new methods and techniques to learn in order to better reach and teach our students.

The inspiration for writing this book comes from our firm belief in children and their ability to succeed when provided with the proper instruction, intervention, and support, as well as the tenacity of committed parents and teachers to do what it takes to help students succeed. During our years in the classroom, we have watched students struggle with written words and suddenly make the exciting reading connection. We have seen children who adamantly avoided reading become avid readers. Parents have shared their worries and stories with us as they have continually looked for ways to help their children.

Technique and methodology are very important in teaching children with dyslexia. Humor, flexibility, and an understanding of each student's unique strengths and weaknesses are also significant in effectively teaching children with learning challenges. Students with dyslexia need the encouragement of parents and teachers, along with interventions that will enable them to achieve academic success.

A wealth of information has come to light about how children learn and the nature of reading disabilities, thanks to the work of many dedicated scientists and researchers. Newly developed reading materials, modern technology, and ongoing research continue to help those who teach students with dyslexia.

It is an exciting time to be working with students who have dyslexia, but this work places many demands on educators and parents. In this book, we have created an easy-to-use, up-to-date reference for parents, teachers, and other professionals who work with dyslexic students. Our goal is to present practical information and collect useful ideas and resources in one place. Many topics in this book lend themselves to extensive explanations. We have attempted to present as much as we can on specific topics in a concise format while encouraging the reader to explore topics further by making use of the resources that are shared throughout the book and listed at the end of each section.

We hope that you find this book to be a valuable resource, and we wish you and your children with dyslexia much success as you meet the challenges ahead.

SANDRA F. RIEF AND JUDITH M. STERN

The Dyslexia Checklist

1

BASIC INFORMATION ON DYSLEXIA

Introduction

Resources

Introduction

Knowledge about dyslexia continues to be updated and clarified. Research, better assessment tools, professional training, and availability of effective intervention programs all contribute to a positive outlook for today's students with dyslexia.

An understanding of both the diagnosis and the treatment of dyslexia will help parents and educators work together with students who have the disorder to maximize students' school success.

1.1 Clarifying the Terms *Dyslexia* and *Learning Disabilities*

Question: My fourth-grade child was diagnosed at school as having learning disabilities. He had great trouble learning the letters of the alphabet and their sounds when he was younger. Reading is a struggle. When he reads, it is slow and very frustrating for him. His spelling is so poor, it's hard to decipher what he writes. My friend told me it sounds like dyslexia. Could this be?

- The answer to the preceding question is yes. *Dyslexia* refers to a language-based learning disability in basic reading skills and spelling. The problems of children with dyslexia most commonly stem from difficulty in processing speech sounds within words and making the connection between sounds and written symbols—letters and patterns of letter combinations—that represent sounds in words.

- Most school districts throughout the United States typically do not use the term *dyslexia*. Some states, like Texas, now do.

- Under the Individuals with Disabilities Education Act (IDEA), the federal special education law, there are thirteen categories of disabilities. "Specific learning disabilities" is one of those categories. *Specific learning disabilities* (SLD) or *learning disabilities* (LD) are the terms typically used in schools.

- *Learning disabilities* is an umbrella term that describes specific problems with processing information and learning skills. Dyslexia is one of the disabilities that is included in *learning disabilities*.

- Dyslexia is the most common learning disability. Approximately 80 percent of students identified as having learning disabilities who qualify for special education have reading disabilities (dyslexia).

Definition of Dyslexia

The International Dyslexia Association (2008a) defines dyslexia as "a specific learning disability that is neurobiological in origin. It is characterized by difficulties with accurate and/or fluent word recognition and by poor spelling and decoding abilities. These difficulties typically result from a deficit in the phonological component of language that is often unexpected in relation to other cognitive abilities and the provision of effective classroom instruction. Secondary consequences may include problems in reading comprehension and reduced reading experience that can impede growth of vocabulary and background knowledge" (adopted by the board of the International Dyslexia Association, November 2002, and the National Institutes of Health, 2002).

Commonly Accepted Descriptions of Dyslexia

- *Dyslexia* is a Greek word meaning "poor language."
- Dyslexia is a language-based disorder that involves weaknesses in phonological awareness, word decoding, and the ability to do rapid naming (quickly name common items or symbols such as colors, numbers, and familiar objects) and quick recall.
- Dyslexia is a brain-based disorder that causes difficulty in using and processing linguistic (speech) and symbolic (letter) codes—that is, letter-sound correspondence.
- Primary characteristics of dyslexia include
  - Difficulty in decoding individual words
  - Slow, inaccurate oral reading—poor reading fluency
  - Spelling weaknesses

Often, dyslexia produces difficulties in other reading and language areas such as reading comprehension, vocabulary, and written language. Individuals with dyslexia exhibit these characteristics to varying degrees, but the characteristics frequently appear in some combination.

What Are Learning Disabilities?

The National Center for Learning Disabilities (NCLD, 2009) defines a learning disability (LD) as "a neurological disorder that affects the brain's ability to receive, process, store and respond to information. The term *learning disability* is used to describe the seeming unexplained difficulty a person of at least average intelligence has in acquiring basic academic skills. These skills are essential for success at school and work, and for coping with life in general. LD is not a single disorder. It is a term that refers to a group of disorders" (n.p.).

- Learning disabilities are neurologically based problems with processing information. These affect one or more processes of input (taking in), integrating (organizing, sequencing, remembering), and output (expression) of the information.

- The problems associated with learning disabilities interfere with one or more of the following: learning reading, writing, or math, and may affect a person's ability to speak, listen, reason, recall, or organize information.

- Children with learning disabilities have difficulties with learning and performing particular skills, and demonstrate underachievement in certain academic areas. For those with dyslexia, the particular skill deficits and underachievement are predominantly in reading and spelling.

- Learning disabilities (including dyslexia) are called hidden disabilities because they are not visible and are not physically obvious.

- Specific learning disabilities are unexpected in relation to a child's age and cognitive and academic abilities. One would not expect the problems the child is experiencing in learning, given his or her average or above-average intellect and other skills and abilities.

- There are school districts that, in practice, do not require average or above-average measured intelligence in order to be classified as learning disabled.

- Federal special education law (IDEA, 2004) defines a *specific learning disability* as "a disorder in one or more of the basic psychological processes involved in understanding or in using language, spoken or written, which may manifest itself in an imperfect ability to listen, think, speak, read, write, spell, or do mathematical calculations. . . ."

- The law's definition also states that the term *specific learning disability* "does not include a learning problem that is primarily the result of visual, hearing, or motor disabilities, of mental retardation, of emotional disturbance, or of environmental, cultural, or economic disadvantage" (United States Code [20 U.S.C. §1401 (30)]).

1.2 Important Facts and General Information About Dyslexia

- Estimates of the number of people in the United States with dyslexia vary from 5 to 17 percent of the population.
- Approximately 3 to 4 percent of students in U.S. schools receive special education services for a reading disability. Far more children who have dyslexia do not receive special education.
- Dyslexia is not caused by
  - Poor parenting or lack of educational opportunities
  - Poor teaching or type of reading instruction
  - Environmental factors
  - Visual or hearing problems
  - Lack of motivation
- Dyslexia affects people all over the world.
- Dyslexia is a lifelong condition. However, intervention can have a very positive impact on a person's ability to read and write.
- Contrary to what many people believe, children with dyslexia do not see letters and words backward. Letter reversals (*b*/*d*, *p*/*q*), as well as errors in directionality and sequencing of letters within words (*was*/*saw*, *on*/*no*), are common in young children with and without dyslexia but may be symptomatic of dyslexia after the early grades.
- Dyslexia is found in both boys and girls in similar numbers, although it is more commonly diagnosed in boys.
- Many characteristics and areas of difficulty are commonly associated with dyslexia. (See Checklists 1.3 and 1.5.) However, each person has his or her own combination of strengths and weaknesses, and the areas of weakness may vary from mild to severe.

- Early identification and intervention (that is, when a child is in kindergarten through second grade) are most effective in preventing reading problems.

- Research shows that with appropriate early intervention, 75–90 percent of children who are at-risk readers can overcome many of their difficulties and increase their reading skills to an average level.

- Although early identification and intervention provide the greatest chances for success, most children with reading disabilities are not diagnosed until they are in the middle or upper elementary grades.

- Many children, teens, and adults with dyslexia go undiagnosed, particularly those with mild degrees of dyslexia. Many fall through the cracks of their school system and never receive the specialized instruction they need to build reading competency. Remediation is more difficult as a person gets older, when remediation must be more intensive in order to overcome years of reading failure. However, it is never too late to help almost anyone with dyslexia learn to read and improve skills.

- Students with dyslexia may have been evaluated at some point but did not meet the eligibility criteria at that time for special education and related services.

- Research tells us what type of instruction is necessary for students with dyslexia and what works best in teaching them to read. (See Checklist 1.10.)

- Dyslexia is not a developmental lag that will eventually go away. Waiting to intervene does not benefit a child.

- Children as young as four or five years old who are at risk for reading problems can be identified through reliable screening measures of phonological awareness and other language-based tasks. Once diagnosed, they can receive early intervention.

- Dyslexia and other learning disabilities may coexist with conditions or disorders, such as speech and language disorders or attention-deficit/hyperactivity disorder (ADHD), that require diagnosis and intervention. It is estimated that 20–40 percent of people with dyslexia also have ADHD.

Causes

- Dyslexia is an inherited neurological condition that often runs in families because there seems to be a genetic basis for this disorder. Between one-third and one-half of children with dyslexia have a family member with dyslexia. A parent or older family member may have never been diagnosed, but the existence of dyslexia can be inferred from a lifelong history of struggle with basic reading and spelling skills.
- Research indicates that dyslexia is the result of a brain difference in the "wiring" of the neural pathways and parts of the brain that are related to language functioning and reading.
- Researchers have found that people with dyslexia may use different and less efficient parts of the brain when doing reading tasks. (See Checklist 1.4.)

Risk Factors

Reading disabilities are associated with a number of problems and risk factors:

- Academic failure and dropping out of school. (Without appropriate intervention, youth and adults with dyslexia are at much higher risk than the rest of the population.)
- Unemployment

- Underemployment (holding a job that is below a person's capabilities or aspirations)
- Emotional or mental health issues, such as depression, related to frustration and low self-esteem
- Other learning or social problems
- Altercations with the law. (A high number of juvenile offenders and prison inmates—60 to 80 percent—have reading problems.)

1.3 Signs and Symptoms of Dyslexia

Because children vary in their development, parents and teachers are not always sure about signs that may indicate the possibility of dyslexia. Rather than looking at individual symptoms, parents and teachers need to look for clusters of symptoms that may indicate the need for an evaluation for dyslexia and other learning disabilities. Children should be watched from early childhood on; identification and intervention at any age is preferable to no treatment at all.

Early risk factors for dyslexia include the following:

Genetics

- Family history of learning disabilities (history of reading problems in parents or siblings)
- Being adopted. (Adopted children have higher rates of learning disabilities.)

Infancy

- Low birth weight; prematurity
- Low Apgar score
- Frequent ear infections that may have affected hearing

Symptoms that may indicate the existence of a learning disability such as dyslexia include difficulties with these:

Motor or Perceptual Skills

- Fine motor skills (using scissors) or gross motor skills (hopping)
- Drawing
- Copying from board or book to paper
- Pencil grip

- Directionality (left and right, up and down)
- Recognizing differences in similar-looking letters, numerals, and words

Language Skills

- Language or speech development
- Receptive language (understanding language)
- Expressive language (ability to communicate thoughts and needs using words)
- Understanding directions
- Use of correct grammar and syntax
- Listening comprehension
- Understanding metaphors, idioms, or words with multiple meanings
- Word retrieval (ability to quickly and accurately pull words from memory)
- Fluency when expressing ideas
- Vocabulary

Early Literacy or Pre-reading Skills

- Understanding that sounds make words
- Rhyming
- Identifying the beginning, middle, and ending sounds in spoken words
- Recognizing, blending, and separating individual sounds within words
- Letter recognition (lowercase and capital)
- Learning the corresponding sounds for letters
- Awareness that we read from left to right and top to bottom of page
- Ability to read and write child's own name

Reading

- Learning the sounds that correspond to letters and letter combinations
- Sounding out (decoding) words
- Differentiating between letters or words that look similar (*p* and *q*, *there* and *three*)
- Recognizing and remembering high frequency or sight words, words such as *said*, *they*, and *she*
- Accuracy (adding or omitting words or parts of words)
- Fluency (reading with ease, speed, and expression)
- Comprehension of text
- Maintaining place while reading

Writing

- Sequencing letters correctly within words
- Copying with accuracy
- Mechanics (correct use of capitalization and punctuation)
- Spelling
- Planning and organizing ideas for writing
- Expressing ideas in complete sentences
- Proofreading skills
- Legible handwriting and appropriate spacing of words
- Staying within the margins of a page and writing on the line
- Aligning numbers in columns when doing math problems

As children develop, symptoms may become more notable. With increased academic demands, problems tend to surface. Additional signs to look for include the following:

Preschool and Kindergarten

- Problems with pronouncing words correctly
- Delayed language and vocabulary development

- Difficulty in reciting the alphabet and days of the week sequentially
- Difficulty with quickly naming things (colors, shapes, familiar objects or animals) when shown pictures or objects
- Frustration with coloring, pasting, cutting with scissors

Grades 1–4

- Slowness in learning the connection between letters and sounds
- Letter reversals (*b/d*) and inversions (*u/n*)
- Lack of a systematic approach to sounding out words
- Difficulty in reading words (by sight and by decoding)
- Frustration with reading tasks
- Good comprehension of material that is read to the child as opposed to text that the child tries to read independently
- Problems with recalling facts
- Difficulty in learning math facts, especially multiplication tables
- Problems with math symbols (confuses signs of operation such as $+$, $-$)
- Problems with understanding time concepts (before, after; telling time)
- Problems in understanding directions

Grades 5–8

- Weak decoding skills; slowness in figuring out multisyllabic words
- Poor sight word vocabulary
- Difficulty in learning spelling strategies such as root words, affixes, spelling patterns

- Poor oral reading; lack of fluency
- Difficulty with word problems in math
- Problems with recalling facts
- Good self-expression orally, but not in writing

High School

- Poor spelling
- Poor written composition
- Avoidance of reading or writing assignments
- Incorrect reading of information
- Trouble with summarizing
- Poor memory skills
- Slow work speed
- Problems with organizing work and managing assignments
- Difficulty with performing in classes that have reading and writing demands
- Difficulty in learning a foreign language

See Checklist 1.5 for additional information on signs and symptoms of problems that are common in dyslexia and other learning disabilities.

1.4 Decades of Research: What We Now Know About Dyslexia

During the past twenty-five years, scientists in the field of reading have done extensive research on how children learn to read, who is at risk of developing reading problems, and interventions for those who struggle with reading. The findings have helped shed light on some causes of dyslexia and have helped define effective instruction and programs for preventing and remediating reading impairment. As researchers learn more about how the brain functions during the reading process, they develop a better understanding of differences in the brains of people with dyslexia. From these findings have come important guidelines for teaching reading effectively to children with dyslexia.

Research sponsored by the National Institute of Child Health and Development is the source of much of what we now understand about reading acquisition and reading disabilities. Recent research on dyslexia that is of particular interest to parents and educators is presented here. Additional information and resources can be found at the end of this section.

- There is a neurological basis for dyslexia. Dyslexia is a brain-based disorder.
- The Connecticut Longitudinal Study, led by Sally Shaywitz, was begun in 1978 in order to study how children learn to read. The researchers looked at both good and poor readers. Shaywitz (2003, p. 28), in her book *Overcoming Dyslexia*, noted that the study helped point out that "reading difficulties occur along a continuum," which is important to know in diagnosing children with dyslexia as well as delivering appropriate intervention services.
- Researchers now use a technology called *functional magnetic resonance imaging* (fMRI) in order to look at the brain at work (for example, while a subject performs a reading task). Research shows that the brain's left hemisphere is involved in most reading activity.

- In the brain's left hemisphere, three regions function together during the reading process.
  - In the front region, phonemes are processed.
  - The region of the brain behind the front region is involved in connecting sounds to the letters that represent them.
  - The third region is used to store words that have been read and learned so that they can later be recognized automatically, without needing to decode sound by sound.
- Brain imaging shows differences in brain activation among good readers compared with people with dyslexia. In good readers, the back of the brain is more activated than the front of the brain during reading.
- Skilled readers make more use of the region of the brain involved in the automatic recognition of words. In poor readers, this area appears to be underactivated, so that a person with dyslexia must work harder to decode each word.
- Researchers found that when people with dyslexia performed reading tasks, the lower front region of the brain was more activated, while the back of the brain was underactivated compared to people without dyslexia.
- In people with dyslexia, there is less activation in the region of the brain involved in the phonetic decoding of words.
- Fluent reading involves activation of the back part of the brain.
- A study by Bennett Shaywitz, Sally Shaywitz, and others (2002) looked at brain activation in children with and without dyslexia as they worked on reading skills such as saying names or sounds of letters, sounding out pseudo-words, and sounding out real words.
  - Children without dyslexia had more activation in areas of the brain that are typically involved in reading than did children with dyslexia.

- • Children who decoded words well had greater activation in areas of the left hemisphere that are important for reading than did those who had dyslexia.
- Teaching children phonological awareness skills as well as phonics and fluency strategies helps activate the region of the brain involved in automatic word recognition.
- Research has shown that instruction in phonemic awareness and reading skills that is intense, explicit, and systematic is considered to have an impact on helping to "rewire" the brain of a person with dyslexia.
- In evaluating instructional strategies that are effective in teaching reading, researchers concluded that teachers must use assorted strategies in order to meet the varied needs of students with dyslexia. Focusing on just one area of reading, one program, or one type of teaching is less effective in helping dyslexic students improve their reading skills.
- Children in kindergarten with weak skills in phonemic awareness are at greater risk for later reading problems than their peers.
- Early identification of dyslexia is important because the brains of young children are "much more plastic . . . and potentially more malleable for the rerouting of neural circuits" (Shaywitz, 2003).
- Scientists have identified genetic markers for dyslexia. Genetic causes are believed to be linked to about half of the risk for reading disabilities.
- Students with dyslexia commonly have problems with phonological awareness. They have difficulty segmenting words into individual phonemes. Students need direct instruction in order to develop these skills. Emphasis on this type of instruction helps to compensate for a main deficit in regard to reading ability.
- Children who are taught to distinguish the separate phonemes that make up words show growth in their reading skills.

- The National Reading Panel was formed in 1997 in order to review the research that had been done on teaching reading. The panel reviewed thousands of studies. Their recommendations, based on research conclusions about how reading should be taught, and found in their report of April 2000, included these findings:

  - Phonemic awareness and systematic phonics should be taught.

  - Guided oral reading is an effective strategy for increasing reading fluency. Children receive guidance and feedback as they read aloud. The goal is to train children to read efficiently and fluently.

  - Children need instruction in reading comprehension techniques and application of strategies so that they will be able to understand the material they read.

  More findings and recommendations from the National Reading Panel can be found at http://www.nichd.nih.gov/publications/nrp/smallbook.cfm, http://www.reading.org/downloads/resources/nrp_summary.pdf, and throughout the checklists in Section Two.

- Remedial work in reading with children who have dyslexia, using research-based programs, helps activate areas of the brain that are involved in reading. Training in reading skills can cause changes in how areas of the brain function.

- See Checklist 1.10 for a description of the criteria established by research to be effective in teaching children to read.

1.5 Other Common Problems

Children and adults with dyslexia often have other learning disabilities and weaknesses in addition to the core difficulties with phonological processing. It is common for people with dyslexia to have coexisting disorders (such as ADHD, dysgraphia, or speech-language problems) or other related problems (such as low self-esteem). Each individual has his or her own combination of strengths and weaknesses and to varying degrees. In addition to signs and symptoms described in Checklist 1.3, difficulties may exist in some of the following areas:

- *Memory*: the ability to hold information in mind long enough to work with it and act on it (working memory); the recall of information recently presented (short-term memory); and retrieving information that has been stored in long-term memory. Children with learning disabilities generally have memory problems to some degree (mild to severe), which can cause difficulty with the following:
  - Remembering words and names
  - Learning rote information by heart (facts or other data for a test)
  - Remembering reading reading and spelling words, especially phonetically irregular or "sight words" such as *was, said, because*. The child may approach these like new words each time they are seen.
  - Remembering and following through on teacher instructions
  - Keeping ideas in mind long enough to remember what one wants to say
  - Learning and being able to quickly recall math facts, particularly multiplication tables
  - Memorizing lines for a play or performance

- Remembering to bring materials needed for homework and turn in assignments
- Performing math problems that require juggling numbers and information mentally while working through problems
- Written composition—holding ideas in mind long enough to manipulate them mentally and get them down on paper

- *Sequencing:* the ability to perceive and control a series of information. Children with learning disabilities often have problems with learning or recalling at an automatic level a sequence of letters, sounds, numbers, and other information. Students with this weakness may have difficulty with the following:
  - Reading words accurately with sounds in correct sequence
  - Following a series of verbal directions
  - Sequencing letters or syllables correctly in a word when spelling (for example, writing "gril" for "girl" or "aminal" for "animal")
  - Skip counting (3, 6, 9, 12)
  - Learning sequences such as the alphabet, months of the year, counting forward or backward
  - Confusing the order of events (for example, summarizing stories in the wrong order)
  - Learning phone numbers and series of numerals
  - Writing in sequence, for example, writing 319 instead of 931
  - Following procedures that involve a sequence of steps and directional order (for example, long division)
  - Writing letters and numbers without a model to refer to (recalling the sequence of pencil strokes needed to form letters or numerals correctly)

- *Executive functioning:* the management functions ("overseers") of the brain—self-directed actions individuals use to help maintain control of themselves and accomplish goal-directed behavior. Children and teens with developmental delays in executive functions often are developmentally immature in the following areas:
  - Self-management and self-regulation skills
  - Working memory
  - Time awareness and time management
  - Planning and organizing skills (particularly for long-term assignments and projects)
  - Ability to get started (activate) and begin tasks that are not intrinsically motivating
  - Ability to sustain the level of attention, effort, and motivation necessary to get through difficult tasks
  - Metacognition (monitoring one's own thinking processes and learning progress, and applying "fix-up" strategies when not doing well)
- *Processing speed:* the rate at which information is processed. Slower processing speed has nothing to do with intelligence. It is not that someone with this problem is a "slow learner," but that he or she processes information at a slower speed, which may cause difficulties with the following:
  - Automatic word recognition and reading fluency
  - Keeping up with the pace of instruction
  - Responding quickly to teacher questions
  - Following along in class discussions
  - Word retrieval (pulling up from memory the precise words one wants to use when speaking or writing)
  - Naming things rapidly and automatically
  - Completing work in a timely manner (class assignments and homework)

- Writing (letter formation and handwriting, spelling, getting ideas on paper, written composition)

Motor Skills and Coordination

- *Gross motor skills:* skills that use the large muscles in one's arms and legs. Children with gross motor weaknesses often have difficulty with the following:
  - Running, skipping, jumping
  - Athletics
  - Physical coordination (clumsiness)
  - Rhythm and balance
  - Social situations. (Other children may reject them in play situations.)
- *Fine motor skills:* skills that use small muscles in the hands and fingers. Children with fine motor weaknesses often have difficulty with:
  - Buttoning, zipping
  - Holding and manipulating a pencil
  - Handwriting

Emotional Functioning

The academic and learning struggles that a child, teen, or adult with learning disabilities faces every day take an emotional toll. It is common for individuals with dyslexia to have problems with the following:

- Low self-esteem (see Checklist 3.5)
- Low tolerance for frustration
- Stress
- Anxiety

- Acting out. (Some children would rather appear "bad" in the eyes of their peers than "dumb.")

Common Coexisting Disorders

Many children with dyslexia have coexisting disorders that need additional intervention. Three common coexisting disorders are as follows:

- *Speech disorders.* Speech therapy can help remediate difficulties with:
  - Articulation (pronouncing sounds in words correctly)
  - Fluency (rate and rhythm of speech)
  - Voice (pitch, loudness, vocal quality)
- *Dysgraphia.* Dysgraphia is a writing disability characterized by poor handwriting and inconsistent spacing of words on the page, difficulty writing on and within the lines and margins, awkward pencil grip and letter formation, and inconsistencies (in size, use of uppercase and lowercase letters, print and cursive), often within a single word or sentence. The physical task of handwriting becomes tedious and frustrating for individuals with dysgraphia. Children with dysgraphia may benefit from occupational therapy or school accommodations.
- *Attention-deficit/hyperactivity disorder.* ADHD is characterized by significant, developmentally inappropriate degrees of inattention, impulsivity, and, in some cases, hyperactivity. Children with ADHD also have executive function deficits, which is a key factor that affects school performance. They often benefit from medical or behavioral intervention as well as school supports and accommodations.

Note: We have each authored a number of books and other resources on ADHD. Visit our Web sites at www.sandrarief.com and www.JudithSternEducationalConsultant.com.

1.6 Common Strengths and Positive Characteristics of People with Dyslexia

In spite of their difficulties, children and adults with dyslexia have many strengths and positive attributes. Knowing that accomplished, highly successful dyslexic adults work in every profession and inhabit every walk of life may motivate children with dyslexia to work hard to reach their goals.

- People with dyslexia may be gifted and talented in various areas—for example, music, arts, athletics, or intellectual pursuits.
- Dyslexic individuals may show special aptitude in visual-spatial thinking or three-dimensional awareness and in professions requiring those abilities (for example, design, architecture, engineering, photography).
- Individuals with dyslexia may have strong technical and mechanical aptitude.
- People with dyslexia may have had to put extra effort into learning and managing well in life; therefore, they may be accustomed to trying hard and fighting barriers in order to achieve success.

See Checklist 1.11 on dual exceptionalities for information on how to meet the needs of children who are gifted and have dyslexia or another disability.

A number of positive characteristics are found in people with dyslexia. Individuals with dyslexia may be

- Persistent
- Innovative
- Imaginative
- Creative
- Inquisitive

- Resourceful
- Resilient
- Inventive
- Good at seeing the big picture
- Problem solvers
- "Out of the box" thinkers with unique points of view
- Strong verbal communicators

1.7 Diagnosing Dyslexia

Determining whether a child or adult has dyslexia requires a formal evaluation (assessment) and diagnosis. This can be done privately through a qualified specialist. The school would provide an evaluation to determine if a child has a reading disability that requires special education and related services.

To be considered eligible for special education and related services in the public schools, students undergo a diagnostic process. Many public school systems are currently using a procedure called *Response to Intervention* to identify students with learning disabilities (see Checklists 5.3 and 5.4). When a student is found to have reading difficulties, intervention would be provided and monitored by the school. If after receiving ongoing intensive, research-based reading instruction at school, the student does not respond with improvement in reading skills, a diagnosis of specific learning disability (which includes dyslexia) may be made.

In young children, evaluating phonological processing has been found to be effective in determining who is at risk for reading and spelling problems. Students with deficits in phonological processing are seen as good candidates for intensive early intervention reading programs.

If a more complete profile of a student is needed, schools may decide to perform a psychoeducational evaluation by administering a full battery of tests. Or parents may hire a private professional to perform an evaluation outside of school.

The goal of this type of evaluation is to look closely at the various learning and cognitive issues that are present. A psychoeducational evaluation provides information about a child's strengths and weaknesses and helps determine whether other difficulties or disabilities exist (for example, other learning disabilities, attention deficit disorder, or emotional disorders). Information is collected from a variety of sources as well as from standardized testing administered individually to the child.

The advantage of this type of evaluation is that it enables parents and educators to look at the overall picture in trying to understand what a child needs in both learning and home environments. Parents and educators are then able to design an intervention plan that meets the specific needs of the student.

Evaluations for learning disabilities

- Are done by a school district to help determine eligibility for special education services through the public school system.
- Involve a team and are generally done by school psychologists and special educators, often with the involvement of speech-language pathologists and reading specialists, in the case of a school-based evaluation.
- Outside of school, may be done by professionals such as licensed psychologists, educational specialists, or mental health counselors. It is important that these professionals have knowledge of reading development and reading disorders, as well as expertise in administering assessments and interpreting assessment data in order to be able to diagnose dyslexia or other learning problems.
- Must use a variety of measures. There is no single test for dyslexia.
- Involve assessment of phonological processing, decoding, word recognition, and spelling skills, among other reading and writing measures.
- Are used to provide formal documentation for eligibility for specific school services as well as accommodations on future tests (such as the SAT).
- Can be performed at any age, preschool through adult.
- Include information provided by parents on family history, medical and developmental information, as well as observations and testing done by professionals.

- Include a review of school history—for example, records of frequent absences, reports of previous interventions, history of difficulty in learning early reading skills, and reports on the student's response to remedial intervention.

- Include a look at the child's language learning (listening and speaking skills).

- May require further evaluations to confirm or reject other issues that surface during the evaluation process (for example, vision, hearing, fine motor, emotional problems).

- Should be followed up with a written report to the student's parents.

Diagnosing Young Adults

Young adults and adults with slow or inaccurate reading fluency may benefit from an evaluation for dyslexia, even if they have never received a diagnosis. Young adults with dyslexia may perform adequately in higher education programs but still have an undiagnosed disability. Diagnosis at any age helps define appropriate forms of educational intervention and useful accommodations.

Understanding Scores on Standardized Testing Reports

Statistical tables are used to describe test scores. Scores are usually reported as *standard scores* and *percentile ranks*.

- A *standard score* shows the relative standing of a score on the bell curve (normal distribution).

- A standard score of 100 represents the statistical average, or *mean*.

- A difference of 15 standard scores or more between subtests or clusters of test items is known as *statistically significant difference*.

- A statistically significant difference means that areas of strength and weakness need to be explained further.

For example, if a child did well in all areas tested, but very poorly in only one area, this would call for a close look at that specific area. If a student did extremely well in math, but average in all other subjects tested, this might call for consideration of giftedness in math.

- A simple way of understanding the meaning of a standard score is by looking at its percentile rank equivalent.

- The percentile rank tells how well a child did on a test or cluster of tests.

- If a child scores at the mean (50th percentile), he or she has done better than 49 out of 100 peers on the test and worse than 50 out of 100 peers chosen at random from the exact peer group.

- Some reports use subtest standard scores that range from 1 to 19, with a mean of 10. In this case a difference of more than two subtest standard scores is statistically significant.

Typical examples of scores are shown in the following table. Each line represents the same score in different forms. For example: a child with a subtest score of 9 has a standard score of 95, at the 37th percentile. This child is doing better than 36 peers, and worse than 63 peers (100 – 37 = 63).

Subtest Standard Score or Scaled Score	Standard Score	Percentile Rank
6	80	9
7	85	16
8	90	25
9	95	37
10	100	50
11	105	63
12	110	75
13	115	84
14	120	90
15	125	95

Tests Used in Diagnosing Dyslexia

This section lists some of the tests that are commonly used in various areas.

Intelligence

Intelligence testing may be performed as part of an evaluation for dyslexia. However, intelligence testing is not currently required by most school systems in the diagnosis of dyslexia. A less formal measure than an intelligence test may be done by public school professionals to determine that a child has adequate cognitive skills. With the adoption of the Response to Intervention model (see Checklist 5.3), different criteria and assessment procedures are now being used by schools to determine eligibility for special education and related services.

A child's reading difficulties may arise for different reasons. For example, a child may have widespread difficulties with verbal thinking and reasoning. Intelligence tests are uniquely suited to uncover an overall problem with verbal and nonverbal abilities. They also can highlight areas of strength, which can be used to help form recommendations for effective remediation. If there is an overall deficit in intelligence, intervention may be different than if overall intelligence were high and the child's reading difficulties were related more to issues such as verbal comprehension, auditory memory, or phonological difficulties.

Intelligence tests generate standard scores, which used to be called *IQ scores*. Intelligence tests most commonly used by psychologists are

- WPPSI (Wechsler Preschool and Primary Scale of Intelligence)
- WISC-IV (Wechsler Intelligence Scale for Children) (ages 6–16)
- WAIS-IV (Wechsler Adult Intelligence Scale) (ages 16–90)

Early Screening

Early screening for the possibility of future reading problems or dyslexia provides an opportunity to closely monitor children's development of reading skills, especially children who might be at risk for reading problems. Screening may determine whether further testing is warranted. Commonly used early screening tests include

- Early Reading Diagnostic Assessment, 2nd edition
- Predictive Assessment of Reading (PAR)
- Dynamic Indicators of Basic Early Literacy Skills (DIBELS)

Achievement and Learning Skills

The following tests are used to evaluate a broad range of skills. These tests contain subtests that examine academic achievement (for example, reading and spelling); memory; and phonological, language, and cognitive skills.

- Woodcock-Johnson Tests of Achievement III
- Woodcock-Johnson Tests of Cognitive Ability III
- Wechsler Individual Achievement Test II (WIAT-II)
- Wide Range Achievement Test IV (WRAT-4)
- Kaufman Test of Educational Achievement II (KTEA-II)

Vocabulary Knowledge

Vocabulary skills are an important component of a child's language and learning profile.

- Peabody Picture Vocabulary Test (PPVT)
- Test of Word Knowledge (TOWK)

Memory

Good memory is required for the acquisition and retention of many academic skills, such as recognizing sight words and remembering spelling rules.

- Wechsler Memory Scale III
- Wide Range Assessment of Memory and Learning, 2nd edition (ages 5–17)

Phonological Awareness

Weaknesses in phonological awareness are considered a major feature of dyslexia.

- Comprehensive Test of Phonological Processing (CTOPP)
- Phonological Awareness Test (PAT)

See Checklist 2.1 for other tests of phonological awareness.

Reading Skills

These tests look specifically at a child's reading skills and add further information to that provided by other comprehensive academic batteries.

- Gray Oral Reading Test 4 (GORT 4)
- Gray Silent Reading Test (GSRT)
- Test of Word Reading Efficiency (TOWRE)
- Woodcock Reading Mastery Test
- Nelson Denny Reading Test (grade 9–adult)

Visual-Motor Integration

Visual-motor tests are nonverbal. They measure skills that affect the development of writing.

- Bender Visual-Motor Gestalt Test, 2nd Edition
- Rey-Osterrieth Complex Figure Test
- Developmental Test of Visual-Motor Integration (VMI), 5th Edition

Oral Language

Assessing oral language is important in evaluating overall language functioning, as well as for comparison with a person's written language skills.

- Clinical Evaluation of Language Fundamentals
- Test of Language Development
- Test of Adolescent Language

Written Language
- Test of Written Language, 4th Edition (TOWL-4)

1.8 Research-Based Intervention Programs for Struggling Readers

Many commercial materials are available to help struggling readers, including programs and curriculum for students who need intensive reading intervention. Several programs are listed here, along with contact information. Additional literacy resources are listed at the end of Section Two.

Programs Based on the Orton-Gillingham Method

In the 1930s and 1940s, Samuel Orton and his associate Anna Gillingham developed their highly structured, systematic, multisensory approach to teaching individuals with dyslexia how to break the code of print in order to read and spell. This approach and subsequent variations of the Orton-Gillingham (O-G) method are the basis of many programs that are used in teaching students with dyslexia. The following programs are some of those that were influenced by the O-G method and supported by research:

Alphabetic Phonics, by Aylett Royall Cox, is a curriculum of multisensory instruction in phonemic awareness, reading, spelling, and handwriting at elementary and secondary levels. Available from Educators Publishing Service at www.epsbooks.com.

Barton Reading and Spelling System, by Susan Barton, is an individualized tutoring system and phonics intervention program for children and adults with dyslexia. Available at www.BartonReading.com.

Failure Free Reading Program, by Joseph Lockavitch, is an intervention program for low-performing readers in grades 1–12. The program's goal is to improve sight vocabulary, fluency, and comprehension skills. Available at www.failurefreeonline.com.

Herman Method, by Renee Herman, is a remedial program for struggling readers in grades 3–12. The curriculum encompasses decoding, spelling skills, sight word recognition, and comprehension skills. Available from Sopris West Educational Services, a Cambium Learning Company, at www.store.cambiumlearning.com and from Lexia Learning Systems at www.lexialearning.com.

Institute for Multisensory Education (IMSE) offers a revised and expanded approach based on the Orton-Gillingham method of reading instruction. IMSE programs provide training in phonemic awareness, phonics, vocabulary development, fluency, and comprehension strategies. Available at www.ortongillingham.com.

PhonoGraphix is a multisensory reading and spelling program based on phonemic awareness and alphabetic code knowledge. Instruction begins at age four or five, when children are learning to read. The program is also intended for struggling readers in grades 1–5 and for those diagnosed with a reading disability. Available from Read America, Inc., at www.readamerica.net.

Project Read, by Mary Lee Enfield and Victoria Greene, has three strands: decoding, reading comprehension, and written expression. This program is for children and adolescents in general and in special education. Available from Project Read by Language Circle Enterprises at www.projectread.com.

Slingerland Multisensory Structured Language Instructional Approach, by Beth Slingerland, is an adaptation of the O-G method, designed to teach dyslexic students integrated skills of speaking, reading, writing, and spelling. This is an approach, not a specific program, that can be used by individuals of all ages from primary grades through adult. All language arts skills—oral expression, decoding, reading comprehension, spelling, and written expression—are taught through integrated, multisensory instruction. Available from Slingerland Institute for Literacy at www.slingerland.org.

Spalding Method, by Romalda B. Spalding, is a total language arts approach for teaching students from preschool through eighth grade (general and special education) phonological awareness, phonics, fluency, vocabulary, comprehension, and handwriting. Available from Spalding Education International at www.spalding.org.

Wilson Reading System, by Barbara Wilson, designed for students in grades 2–12, is a complete curriculum for teaching decoding and spelling, beginning with phoneme segmentation. Instruction includes sight word instruction, fluency, vocabulary, oral expressive language, and comprehension. Available from Wilson Language Training at www.wilsonlanguage.com.

Other Research-Based Programs

The programs in this list have been validated by research as effective interventions for struggling readers.

Corrective Reading, by Gary Johnson and Zig Engleman, provides intensive intervention for children in grades 4–12 who read below grade level (general or special education). The program is designed to improve decoding, fluency, and comprehension through scripted lessons and direct instruction. Available from SRA/McGraw-Hill at www.sra4kids.com.

Language! The Comprehensive Literacy Curriculum, by Jane Fell Green, is designed to build the reading, writing, and other language skills of students in grades 3–12 who are struggling readers, writers, speakers, and spellers. Available from Sopris West Educational Services,

a Cambium Learning Company, at http://store
.cambiumlearning.com or www.sopriswest.com.

Lindamood-Bell programs, by Patricia Lindamood, Phyllis
Lindamood, and Nanci Bell, are designed to teach children and adults with dyslexia to read, spell, comprehend language, and express themselves. The Lindamood
Phoneme Sequencing® (LiPS) Program trains children to
be aware of different speech sounds (phonemes) and identify each according to the position of the lips, teeth, and
tongue in making the sound (for example, /p/ /b/ are called
lip poppers and /t/, /d/ are called *tip tappers*). Available from
Lindamood-Bell Learning Process at www.lindamoodbell
.com.

PALS Reading (Peer Assisted Learning Strategies),
by Doug Fuchs and Lynn Fuchs, is a structured whole-
classroom reading program for preschool through twelfth
grade. The focus in preschool is on letter names, letter
sounds, first-sound identification, and phonological awareness. In kindergarten, children practice letter-sound correspondence, decoding, phonological awareness, and sight
words. First-grade PALS Reading emphasizes decoding
and reading fluently. In grades 2–6, activities build fluency
and comprehension. High school PALS Reading is similar.
Available from Vanderbilt Kennedy Center for Research
on Human Development at http://kc.vanderbilt.edu/pals/.

Quick Reads, by Elfrieda Hiebert, is designed to improve
reading fluency and has comprehension, vocabulary, and
background knowledge elements. The program, for students in grades 2–4, consists of short informational texts
that are read quickly for meaning. Each level sequentially
develops reading rate. Texts are designed so that they can
be read in one minute. Available at http://quickreads.org.

Read Naturally, by Candyce Ihnot, is a fluency development program for individuals of all ages and abilities that

uses teacher modeling, repeated readings, and monitoring of progress. Students choose from stories at their assigned level and listen as a proficient reader models correct reading. They then read the story with a timer until they reach a predetermined goal for their rate. Students chart their own progress. Available at www.readnaturally.com.

Reading Mastery, by Siegfried Engelmann and colleagues, comes in two versions: *Reading Mastery Classic,* levels I and II, for grades K–3, and *Reading Mastery Plus*, an integrated reading and language program for grades K–6. This program of direct instruction is designed for children at high risk for reading problems. Teachers follow a scripted lesson plan that breaks concepts into smaller subskills. Available from Science Research Associates (SRA) at www.sraonline.com or www.sra4kids.com.

REWARDS (Reading Excellence: Word Attack and Rate Development Strategies), by Anita Archer, Mary Gleason, and Vicky Vachon, is designed as an intense intervention for students in grades 4–12 who are not accurate or fluent oral readers. The intermediate program is for grades 4–6, and the secondary program is for grades 6–12. Students learn strategies for decoding long words and increasing fluency, particularly in content-area passages. Available from Sopris West Educational Services, a Cambium Learning Company, at http://store.cambiumlearning.com.

Sounds Sensible and **SPIRE,** by Sheila Clark-Edmands, are two programs for at-risk or struggling readers.

* *Sounds Sensible*, for children in preschool through first grade, provides direct instruction and activities in phonological awareness and beginning phonics. *SPIRE*, for students in preschool through eighth grade, is a multisensory program that incorporates total language instruction—phonological awareness, phonics, fluency,

vocabulary, spelling, handwriting, and comprehension. Available from Educators Publishing Service at www .epsbooks.com.

Soar to Success, by David Cooper and David Chard, is a K–8 intensive reading intervention program that includes assessment and progress monitoring. Goals for grades 3–8 include accelerating reading ability and helping students apply comprehension and decoding strategies. Available from Houghton Mifflin at www.eduplace.com/ intervention/soar/.

Spell Read, developed by Kay McPhee, is a one-year small-group reading intervention program that focuses on phonological automaticity and reading fluency, vocabulary instruction, and opportunities for writing. It is administered in grades 2–12 in daily pull-out programs led by specially trained teachers. Available from Kaplan at www.kaplank12.com.

Research-Validated Intervention Software

Earobics is reading intervention software supported by multimedia materials and student-guided activities. Interactive games provide individualized, explicit instruction in all areas of reading for students in preschool to third grade. The program automatically adjusts according to a student's strengths and weaknesses. Progress monitoring is included. There are two versions: *Foundations* for children in preschool through first grade, and *Connections* for students in second and third grade and for other struggling readers. Available at www.earobics.com.

Fast ForWord, by Paula Tallal and David Merzenich, is a software program designed to train the ability to hear phonemes (speech sounds) at increasingly faster speeds over six to eight weeks. It is not a reading intervention program but may benefit development and strengthening of language processing skills. Available from Scientific Learning Company at http://www.scilearn.com/.

Headsprout Early Reading is a supplemental online reading program for children in preschool through second grade who are at the beginning stages of learning to read. The program provides individualized instruction through interactive activities. Available at www.headsprout.com.

Lexia Reading is a software program that provides intensive, structured practice that builds reading skills at different levels, covering Early Reading (preschool through first grade), Primary Reading (preschool through third grade), and Strategies for Older Students (sixth through twelfth grade). The program includes a management system with reporting features. Available from Lexia Learning Systems at www.lexialearning.com.

Read 180, by Ted Hasselbring, Kate Kinsella, and Kevin Feldman, is a multimedia instructional software program that provides intensive, differentiated practice in reading, writing, and vocabulary skills. The program analyzes, tracks, and reports on student accuracy. Available from Scholastic at http://teacher.scholastic.com/products/read180.

Read, Write, & Type! is a systematic reading and writing software program for six- to eight-year-olds who are just learning to read and for older children who are struggling readers and writers. The program teaches awareness of English phonemes (speech sounds) and the ability to associate each phoneme with a letter or pair of letters and finger strokes on a keyboard. The program also tracks student progress. Available at www.readwritetype.com or www.talkingfingers.com.

Waterford Early Reading Program, by Waterford Institute, a multiple-year program of instruction for children in preschool through second grade, provides individualized, self-paced instruction as well as reports. The program uses classroom lessons and take-home materials that are tailored to each student's reading level in order to promote reading, writing, and typing, as well as other language and literacy skills. Available at www.waterfordearlylearning .org.

Wiggleworks is interactive multimedia software that helps students in preschool through third grade develop reading, writing, listening, and speaking skills by presenting interactive books with reading support. The software provides instruction in phonemic awareness, phonics, vocabulary, comprehension, and writing activities. Available from Scholastic at www.scholastic.com.

A number of reading programs have been evaluated, including several from this checklist. See the following resources for more information.

- The Florida Center for Reading Research reports on supplemental intervention reading programs, comprehensive intervention reading programs, and Tier 3 Response to Intervention programs.

  www.fcrr.org
- U.S. Department of Education, Institute of Education Sciences, What Works Clearinghouse

  http://ies.ed.gov/ncee/wwc/reports/
- John Hopkins University, Best Evidence Encyclopedia

  www.bestevidence.org
- Oregon Reading First Center: Review of Supplemental and Intervention Programs

  http://oregonreadingfirst.uoregon
  .edu/inst_curr_review_si.html

1.9 What Children with Dyslexia Need from Parents and Teachers

- Hope and optimism about the future and their ability to achieve their goals
- Belief in them
- Ongoing support, encouragement, and advocacy
- Determination to do what it takes to help them succeed
- Expert teachers who are knowledgeable and skilled in teaching students with reading disabilities and use of research-based instructional methods
- Accommodations and modifications to enable success in the general education curriculum
- Strong efforts to prevent problems (for example, early identification of needs and appropriate interventions)
- The necessary degree and intensity of remediation to build skills and accelerate academic achievement
- Flexibility and willingness to make necessary adaptations
- Knowledge about dyslexia (what it is and is not) and awareness of strategies and interventions that are proven to help
- Willingness to take advantage of available resources (books, training, conferences, Web sites) to obtain current information and support
- Programs that fit their individual needs, so that they are not forced to try to fit into existing programs that are inappropriate to their needs
- Reminders, when they are frustrated, that they have many strengths and talents and that their difficulties are not due to a lack of intelligence
- Assistance in building confidence and self-esteem
- Avoidance of words that cause humiliation, embarrassment, or hurt (such as *lazy, unmotivated, careless*)

- Efforts to nurture, develop, and utilize their strengths, interests, and talents
- Numerous opportunities to participate in activities that match their interests or talents (for example, art, music, theater, athletics)
- Ability to gently let go when they show the willingness and ability to handle something independently
- Close communication and teamwork (between home and school, as well as with tutors, therapists, or other service providers)

1.10 Key Instructional Components and Interventions for Students with Dyslexia

Students with signs and symptoms of dyslexia should have an appropriate evaluation in order to assess their phonological processing, literacy skills, and other learning strengths and weaknesses. Early diagnosis and intervention are always the most beneficial as there is greater opportunity to provide the help and instruction needed for children to develop their skills, and prevent many problems in learning to read and write. However, at any age or grade, a student can learn when provided with effective, well-designed instruction and materials. Students with dyslexia need specific kinds of instruction in order to maximize their learning.

Key Elements of Instructional Design for Students with Dyslexia

- *Direct and explicit:* Each skill, rule of language, and strategy for reading and spelling words must be taught clearly and directly, without assuming that the student has even the most basic foundational skills or background knowledge about the English written language. Elements of direct instruction include
  - Introducing one new skill or focus of instruction at a time
  - Specific procedures for introducing, practicing, and reviewing skills
  - Explicit teacher modeling
  - A high degree of guided practice in which the teacher frequently checks for students' understanding
  - Providing immediate corrective feedback

- Ongoing review and checking for retention and mastery of previously taught skills
- Reteaching as needed
- Independent practice
- Active student engagement throughout the lesson

- *Systematic and structured:* Students with dyslexia typically have gaps in their understanding of how the English written language system works. They need to be taught a systematic scope and sequence (coverage and organization) of skills, starting at a beginning level to ensure mastery of foundational skills and filling in holes in a student's repertoire of skills. Each lesson gradually builds on previously taught skills or concepts, and students are moved along at an appropriate individual pace.

An example of a systematic scope and sequence of reading skills for early instruction would be teaching

- Single consonants before two- and three-letter consonant blends
- One vowel at a time—for example, introducing *short a* words first, and progressing through reading and spelling one-syllable words with all the short vowels
- Phonetically regular short-vowel words before phonetically regular long-vowel words—for example, *hat, mad* before *hate, made*
- One new syllable pattern or type at a time—for example, *r*-controlled syllables (bird, hurt), double vowel syllables (team, road)
- Phonetically regular words before irregular words
- One-syllable words before multisyllabic words

Instruction is organized in a manner that

- Enables the learner to see patterns and regularities in order to make connections

- Minimizes confusion
- Teaches skills and small amounts of new information in steps, each step building on the prior one
- Provides frequent review and practice
- *Multisensory:* Regardless of the program used, teaching children with dyslexia requires the use of multisensory techniques, which make learning more memorable. Students with dyslexia usually learn best when instruction incorporates some combination of auditory, visual, and tactile-kinesthetic input as well as many opportunities to practice.

Following are some examples of multisensory approaches for teaching the letter *s* (the sound and the symbol):

- The letter *s* is presented as a snake drawn in the shape of the letter *s*. This technique gives a memory clue for the shape of the letter and the beginning sound of *snake*.

- Students are asked to look in the mirror while making the /s/ sound, which is like a snake hissing (ssssssss). Attention is focused on the mouth and tongue position while saying the sound.

- The teacher points out that /z/ and /s/ have the same mouth and tongue position, but /z/ is voiced, meaning that vibration can be felt when placing one's hand over the vocal chords. The /s/ is unvoiced; no vibration is felt in vocal chords when making the /s/ sound.

- Students are shown a hand signal for a slithering snake as a prompt for making the /s/ sound: making a fist with one hand and sticking out the thumb (like a snake's tongue). Next, students make the hand motion of the snake slithering up and down with its tongue out while hissing the ssssssss sound.

- Students practice tracing the letter *s*, writing it multiple times in various textures, making the hand motion of the snake while saying sssssss.

See the resource *Alphabet Learning Center Activities Kit* (Fetzer & Rief, 2000) for more teaching activities using this method.

What Students with Dyslexia Need to Be Taught

- *Phonemic awareness:* the sound structure of our language—how to recognize, manipulate, blend, and segment individual speech sounds in words. (See Checklist 2.1.)

- *Phonics and decoding skills:* the correspondence of graphemes (letters) and phonemes (sounds); how to analyze unknown words through sounding out and other strategies. (See Checklists 2.2 and 2.3.)

- *Components of language:* vocabulary, word usage, prefixes, suffixes, and other parts of words that carry meaning (morphemes). (See Checklists 2.3 and 2.6.)

- *Fluency:* how to read words automatically. (See Checklists 2.5 and 3.6.)

- *Comprehension strategies:* how to derive meaning from text. (See Checklists 2.7, 3.6, and 4.8.)

- *Spelling skills and strategies:* using their sounding-out skills and word structure awareness to encode or put words they want to use in printed form. (See Checklists 2.4 and 2.8.)

- *Metacognitive strategies:* awareness of their own learning processes—for example, how they learn best; when, where, and how to use specific strategies. (See Checklists 2.7, 2.10, 2.11, 2.12, 3.8, and 4.7.)

Teaching Reading and Writing to Dyslexic Students Requires

- Research-validated curriculum (see Checklist 1.8) that
  - Uses a multisensory, structured approach
  - Is taught directly and explicitly
  - Is structured, systematic, sequential, and cumulative
- Intensity of instruction that is greater than that needed for students without learning problems, including
  - Sufficient time provided for direct skill and strategy instruction
  - Student practice with immediate corrective feedback and reinforcement
  - Instruction provided either one on one or in small groups of students of the same skill level
- Ongoing assessment (informal and formal) and careful monitoring of progress. (Assessment results should guide instruction.)
- New skill sets and concepts that are broken into small, clear steps and repeatedly practiced

1.11 Dual or Multiple Exceptionalities (Gifted and Dyslexic)

Twice exceptional or *dual exceptional* (also referred to as *2e*) students are those who are gifted and also have a disability such as dyslexia or another learning disability, ADHD, or Asperger's syndrome. Some children with dyslexia have multiple exceptionalities. For example, they are gifted, dyslexic, and have ADHD. These children have both very high potential in one or more areas and significant learning challenges in others. A twice exceptional student might, for example, be very advanced in math and well below grade level in reading. Due to lack of awareness, understanding, and appropriate diagnosis, students with dual exceptionalities may fall through the cracks and not receive appropriate services.

Gifted Students

- The federal government's educational definition of gifted and talented students are those "who give evidence of high achievement capability in areas such as intellectual, creative, artistic, or leadership capacity, or in specific academic fields, and who need services or activities not ordinarily provided by the school in order to fully develop those capabilities" (No Child Left Behind Act, Pub. L. No. 107-110, Title IX, Part A, Definitions 22 [2002]; 7802, 20 U.S.C. 22 [2004]).
- States and districts vary in their criteria for identifying gifted students and how to deliver special services, programs, and activities to children meeting eligibility criteria.

Special Challenges for Twice Exceptional Students

- *Being misunderstood.* Disorders such as dyslexia or ADHD are not related to one's intelligence. Someone may be highly intelligent yet have significant learning difficulties. Because they are bright, their underachievement is unfairly attributed to their being lazy, unmotivated, or apathetic.

- *Emotional issues.* Twice exceptional students may be at risk for anxiety or low self-esteem that arises from the frustration of coping with their learning challenges and trying to live up to high expectations (often their own) to excel academically.

- *Being identified as gifted.* Twice exceptional students' disability may mask their giftedness. They may not be evaluated because average academic performance prevents them from being considered candidates for programs for the gifted. Others may be evaluated but not identified as gifted because of poor test-taking skills.

- *Having their disorder diagnosed and treated.* Many gifted children use their intelligence to compensate for their learning difficulties. They may go years without being diagnosed (sometimes into adulthood). Their giftedness masks their disability, but compensating for their disability on their own may take an emotional toll.

- *Receiving appropriate educational programming or services.* Twice exceptional students may not receive the intellectually challenging curriculum or enrichment they need. They are also far less likely to be found eligible for special education programs, related services, or accommodations, particularly when they compensate and perform at grade level.

What Twice Exceptional Students Need

- Proper evaluation and diagnosis
- Enriching experiences beyond the basic school curriculum
- Acceleration in areas of strength (being allowed to move quickly through basic content curriculum that they have already mastered, providing extra time to work on challenging projects of interest)

- A mentor to encourage and guide them
- Teamwork among school and district staff and parents who are working to meet their unique educational needs
- Opportunities to develop their strengths and interests
- The same opportunities that other gifted students receive
- Accommodations for their special needs. (They may be successful in programs for the gifted and advanced placement classes if they are given supports and accommodations, such as assistive technology.)
- Advocacy by parents and teachers

Tips for Parents and Teachers of Twice Exceptional Students

- Be alert to signs of dual or multiple exceptionalities; don't be thrown off by highly discrepant abilities.
- Share observations with each other. Refer students for appropriate diagnostic assessments.
- Seek opportunities to nurture students' talents and showcase their strengths.
- Provide assistance when needed, even though twice exceptional students may have the intellectual ability to do good work.
- Address emotional and self-esteem issues that arise; provide encouragement and support. (See Checklist 3.5.)
- For more information on this topic, investigate these resources:
  - *Twice Exceptional Newsletter* (Glen Ellyn Media) www.2enewsletter.com
  - Uniquely Gifted Resources for Gifted Children with Special Needs www.uniquelygifted.org

- Smart Kids with Learning Disabilities
  www.smartkidswithld.org
- Association for the Education of Gifted Underachieving Students
  www.aegus1.org

Resources

Aylward, E. H., Richards, T. L., Berninger, V. W., Nagy, W. E., Field, K. M., Grimme, A. C., Richards, A. L., Thomson, J. B., & Cramer, S. C. (2003). Instructional treatment associated with changes in brain activation in children with dyslexia. *Neurology, 61*(2), 212–219.

Braaten, E., & Felopulos, G. (2004). *Straight talk about psychological testing for kids.* New York: Guilford Press.

Fetzer, N., & Rief, S. (2000). *Alphabet learning center activities kit.* San Francisco: Jossey-Bass.

Hudson, R., High, L., & Al Otalba, S. (2007). Dyslexia and the brain: What does current research tell us? *Reading Teacher, 60*(6), 506–515.

International Dyslexia Association. (2008a, March). *Just the facts: Definition of dyslexia.* Retrieved July 3, 2009, from www.interdys.org/ewebeditpro5/upload/Definition_Fact_Sheet_3-10-08.pdf

International Dyslexia Association. (2008b, September). *Just the facts: Is my child dyslexic?* Retrieved July 3, 2009, from http://www.interdys.org/ewebeditpro5/upload/Is_My_Child_Dyslexic_9-12-8.pdf

International Dyslexia Association. (2008c, December). *Just the facts: Testing and evaluation.* Retrieved July 3, 2009, from http://www.interdys.org/ewebeditpro5/upload/Testing_and_Evaluation_Fact_Sheet_12-08.pdf

International Reading Association. (2002). *Summary of the (U.S.) National Reading Panel report: Teaching children to read.* Newark, DE: Division of Research and Policy, International Reading Association. Retrieved July 3, 2009, from http://www.reading.org/downloads/resources/nrp_summary.pdf

Kay, M. (Winter, 2002). *Preparation of a psycho-educational evaluation report.* Retrieved July 3, 2009, from http://www.harborhouselaw.com/articles/kay.report.htm

National Center for Learning Disabilities. (2007). *Checklist of LD signs and symptoms.* Retrieved July 3, 2009, from http://www.ncld.org/content/view/447/391/

National Center for Learning Disabilities. (2009). *LD at a glance.* Retrieved July 3, 2009, from http://www.ncld.org/ld-basics/ld-explained/basic-facts/learning-disabilities-at-a-glance

National Institutes of Health, National Institute of Child Health and Human Development. (April 2000). *Report of the National Reading Panel. Teaching children to read: An evidence-based assessment of the scientific research literature on reading and its implications for reading instruction* (NIH Publication No. 00-4769). Washington, DC: U.S. Government Printing Office. Retrieved July 3, 2009, from http://www.nichd.nih.gov/publications/nrp/smallbook.cfm

Rief, S., & Heimburge, J. (2006). *How to reach and teach all children in the inclusive classroom* (2nd ed.). San Francisco: Jossey-Bass.

Shaywitz, B. A., Shaywitz, S. E., Pugh, K. R., Mencl, W. E., Fulbright, R. K., Skudlarksi, P., Constable, R. T., Marchione, K. E., Fletcher, J. M., Lyon, G. R., & Gore, J. C. (2002). Disruption of posterior brain systems for reading in children with developmental dyslexia. *Biological Psychiatry, 52*(2), 101–110.

Shaywitz, S. (1996, November). Dyslexia. *Scientific American, 275*(5), 98–104.

Shaywitz, S. (2003). *Overcoming dyslexia: A new and complete science-based program for reading problems at any level.* New York: Knopf.

Silver, L. B. (2006). *The misunderstood child* (4th ed.). New York: Three Silver Press.

Torgesen, J. K. (2002). The prevention of reading difficulties. *Journal of School Psychology, 40*(1), 7–26.

Wright, P., & Wright, P. D. (2008, September). *Tests and measurements for the parent, teacher, advocate and attorney.* Retrieved July 3, 2009, from http://www.wrightslaw.com/advoc/articles/tests_measurements.html

2

STRATEGIES FOR HELPING WITH READING, LANGUAGE, AND WRITING

Introduction

Resources

Introduction

Reading is a complex process that demands competence in many different skills. Learning to read involves moving from the basic mechanical skills needed to read letters and words to skills that involve understanding the meaning of words, sentences, paragraphs, and chapters. Children move at different rates in developing these skills, and they vary in their abilities to grasp each step.

In the beginning of the process, children must develop phonological awareness, which will enable them to learn the rules of phonics. Decoding strategies and syllabication help readers figure out unfamiliar words systematically. The ability to recognize irregular words in English is necessary in order for reading to proceed smoothly. Reading fluency develops with mastery of the more fundamental skills. Knowledge of vocabulary and comprehension of what has been read are the higher levels of reading competence.

Students with dyslexia may have difficulty mastering some or all of the stages that are necessary in order to become an effective reader. Development may be slow or uneven. Effective teaching, ongoing support, encouragement, and persistence all help the process. Good instruction must focus on all areas of reading in order to be effective. While there is no perfect system or one right way to teach reading to struggling readers, students today can benefit from research and increased knowledge in the field of reading education.

Children with dyslexia typically have significant difficulty with some or many aspects of writing as well as reading. This section contains strategies and supports that teachers, parents, and tutors can provide in reading as well as spelling and throughout the entire writing process (prewriting, composing, revising, and editing). Technology and games to accommodate and motivate students who struggle with reading and writing are also presented.

2.1 Phonological Awareness

Even before entering school, young children begin to develop important skills they will need in order to learn to read. Being able to understand and use the sounds of language prepares children for reading instruction. *Phonological awareness* is a set of skills viewed by educators and researchers as a major precursor to the development of reading skills. Eventually, most young children are able to connect spoken sounds they hear to letters they see, which allows them to learn the reading process.

Dyslexia is marked by difficulty in reading caused by problems with associating oral language and written language and problems with identifying individual speech sounds within words, the order of sounds or syllables, and working with rhyme. All of these are skills that constitute phonological awareness. Dyslexia is viewed as a language processing difficulty at the phonemic level.

Students who have weaknesses in the area of phonological awareness can be expected to struggle in learning to read. These students may require additional instruction as well as different types of instruction.

Understanding Phonological Awareness

- Phonological awareness is the awareness of the sounds of language—speech sounds. It is the understanding that oral language can be broken into component parts in a variety of ways:
  - Sentences into words (The girl ate a cake.)
  - Words into syllables (fan-tas-tic)
  - Words into onset/rime (f-at, fl-at, ch-at)
  - Words into phonemes (sun to /s/u/n/)

- Systematic instruction in phonological awareness can improve pre-reading skills and have a positive impact on a child's ability to learn to read.
- Phonological awareness involves the ability to manipulate sounds in a word by deleting, adding, and substituting syllables or sounds.
- At age four, children should be able to do rhyming activities.
- In kindergarten and first grade, students should be able to
  - Break words apart and blend them by onset and rime (ch-op, r-ink)
  - Blend sounds to form words. For example, students might be asked to blend the individual sounds of /m/ . . . /a/ . . . /n/, saying them quickly as "man."
  - Break words into individual parts. For example, hearing the word *mop*, students can segment the word into individual sounds (phonemes), saying each sound slowly as /m/ . . . /o/ . . . /p/.
  - Delete phonemes. For example, "Say 'rink.' Now say it without the /r/." "Say the word *drip*. Now say it without the /r/."
- As children progress in reading, they continue to use phonological awareness skills as they encounter new words and learn to systematically attack them. These skills are also used as children begin to spell.
- *Phonemic awareness* is a subset of phonological awareness that is directly related to early reading success. It involves understanding that words can be broken into *phonemes* (the smallest units of sound). Phonemes are not the same as the letters or the spelling of a word. For example, the word *bike* has three phonemes or distinct sounds: /b/ī/k/. The word *neighbor* has four phonemes: /n/ā/b/r/.
- Being able to recognize, blend, and separate (segment) individual sounds heard within words are prerequisite skills to

phonics and decoding (reading) words and encoding (spelling) them.

- Phonemic awareness is a set of oral language skills—being able to hear and manipulate language sounds. Phonemic awareness consists of the highest level of phonological awareness skills, involving the ability to

  - Understand that sounds make words.

  - Discriminate (hear the difference between) phonemes (for example, the difference between /p/ and /t/).

  - Identify beginning, medial, and ending sounds of words. (In the word *mad*, the beginning sound is /m/, the medial sound is /a/, and the ending sound is /d/.)

  - Syllabicate words or break them into chunks (re-member, kit-ten).

  - Blend individual sounds together to form a word. (When blended together, the sounds /r/ /e/ /d/ make the word *red*.)

  - Segment or break apart individual sounds within a word. (In the word *must*, we hear the sounds /m/ /u/ /s/ /t/.)

  - Manipulate sounds in words. (In the word *snap*, if we took away the /s/, we would have the word *nap*.)

Sequence of Phonological Awareness Skills

There is a continuum or hierarchy of phonological skills. For example, children first develop a recognition of rhyme before they are able to produce rhyming words, and awareness of bigger parts of words (syllables) precedes awareness of individual sounds within words (phonemes). There is variation in the recommended sequence among researchers, but some suggest the following:

- Word segmentation: differentiating individual words within a sentence. For example, students might be asked how many words are in the sentence "The boy played tag."

- Rhyme recognition: being able to tell when words rhyme (tick, sick, pick)
- Rhyme completion ("It rhymes with 'at' and begins with /m/. What is the word?")
- Rhyme production ("Give me two words that rhyme with *mop*.")
- Syllable blending ("Hun . . . ger—what word is that?")
- Syllable segmentation ("Clap for each syllable in the word *important*.")
- Syllable deletion ("If I say *snowfall* and take away *fall*, what word do I have?")
- Syllable substitution ("If I say *rainbow*, take away *bow*, and add *coat*, what word do I have?")
- Working with words at the phoneme level:
  - Phoneme discrimination: "Which sound do you hear at the end of 'job?' /b/ or /p/?"
  - Phoneme imitation: "Repeat after me: ffff."
  - Phoneme isolation: "What sound do you hear at the beginning of Jenny's name?"
  - Phoneme blending: "What word am I saying: sss iii ttt?"
  - Phoneme segmentation: "Take the word *ran* and say each of its sounds slowly: rrrraaannnn . . . /r/a/n/."
  - Phoneme manipulation (adding, deleting, substituting, transposing).
    "Take the word *hit* and add /s/ to the end. What word do you have?"
    "Take the name *Fred* and take away /f/. What word do you have?"
    "Take the word *pay*, remove /p/ and add /s/. What word do you have?"
    "Take the word *pot* and say it backward. What word do you have?"

Features of Effective Phonological Awareness Instruction

- Models activities for students.
- Moves from larger units of sound (onset-rime) to smaller ones (separate phonemes). It is easier to begin working with words such as b-at; c-at, spl-at to help children create words, then move on to the more complex task of building words from individual phonemes: /s/ĭ/t/.
- Moves from easier activities, such as rhyming, to segmenting and blending.
- In teaching individual sounds, presents the ones that are continuous and easier to say, such as /s/ /m/ /f/, then moves to "stop" sounds, such as /p/ /b/ /k/. The continuous sounds are easier to stretch out orally, so that a child can slide from one sound to the next. When saying /mmm/ /aaa/ /nnn/, the sounds can be held longer than those in a word such as *pat*, in which the first and final sounds cannot be stretched.
- In early activities in segmenting words, focuses on the beginning and ending sounds of words. Students practice identifying beginning and ending sounds heard in words and matching words that have the same beginning or ending sounds, either through listening or through looking at pictures. For example, "Look at this picture. Show me something that starts with the same first sound."
- Uses activities involving manipulatives (for example, blocks or tiles to represent each sound). For example, draw three or four boxes on a piece of paper. Now say words with two, three, or four phonemes. As you say a word slowly, have the child push a block, tile, or penny into a box while each phoneme is said. Say "seal" (three phonemes: /s/ . . . /ē/ . . . /l). As the sounds are stretched out while you say "seal" slowly, the child pushes one tile into a box for /s/, one for the / ē / sound, and one for the /l/ sound. Next, say "frog." *Frog* has

four phonemes, so the child pushes a penny into a box for each phoneme:/f/, /r/, /o/, /g/.

Strategies for Teaching and Reinforcing Phonological Awareness Skills

Children need a great deal of exposure to recognizing rhymes. Listening to rhyming poems and stories, reciting poems that rhyme, and singing rhyming songs provide this experience. Children also need practice in learning to combine individual sounds as well as syllables together in order to form words.

Rhyming

- Ask children to identify words that rhyme in a poem, story, or song.

- Have students make up their own rhymes by adding a word:

   "My name is Billy and I am very ————."

   "I saw a cat who is really ————."

- Play word games that involve rhyme:

   "I am looking in the room at something white that rhymes with tall. What is it?" (wall, ball)

- Create card games or bingo boards. When a child picks a card that rhymes, a match is made.

- Present a child with two words. Ask whether they rhyme.

   Can, fit

   Top, mop

Working with Syllables and Words

- When lining up to leave the room, each child must give a two- or three-syllable word. Or have all students with one-syllable first names line up first, then those with two syllables, and so on.

- Practice activities that involve deletion, substitution, and addition of sounds.

    "If I have the word *still* and take away the /st/, what word is it?"

    "If I have the word *no*, take off the /n/, and put in /g/, what word is it?"

    "Take the word *mail* and add the word *box*; what word is it?"

- Ask children to think of as many words as they can that begin or end with a specific sound.

- Provide practice in blending together three and four sounds to make a word.

    "What word is this? fff-uuu-nnn."

What the Research Tells Us

- There is a strong relationship between phonological awareness and the ability to read well. Deficits in this area that appear in kindergarten are predictive of difficulties in learning to read.

- Reading disabilities not identified by third grade are likely to continue through the elementary school years and beyond.

- Phonological awareness skills can be developed and improved by providing children with systematic instruction.

- Teaching phonological awareness is helpful for children as young as age four and should be well established by the end of first grade.

Screening Tools and Tests for Assessing Phonological Awareness of Young Children

These tools are designed for students in the second part of kindergarten and in first grade:

- Test of Phonological Awareness-Kindergarten (TOPA-K) www.proedinc.com
- Yopp-Singer Test of Phoneme Segmentation (Yopp, 1995)
- DIBELS Phoneme Segmentation Fluency measure (Kaminski and Good, 1996) University of Oregon http://dibels.uoregon.edu
- Phonological Awareness Literacy Screening (PALS) http://curry.edschool.virginia.edu/go/pals/
- Phonological Awareness Test (PAT) Lingui Systems www.linguisystems.com
- Comprehensive Test of Phonological Processing in Reading (CTOPP) Pro-Ed, Inc. www.proedinc.com
- Lindamood Auditory Conceptualization Test (LAC) Pro-Ed, Inc. www.proedinc.com

2.2 Systematic Phonics

Phonics is a type of instruction that teaches the connection between letters and sounds (alphabetic principle). When children learn phonics, they first understand that sounds can be represented in print. Then they are taught to connect sounds with specific letters. Using phonics as a reading strategy, children link letters or a group of letters to each of their spoken sounds, then blend those sounds together to read words. To recognize words with fluency, children need good phonics skills.

Phonics provides readers with a strategy for decoding (analyzing) words by sounding them out. Phonics skills involve combining (blending) individual sounds, as well as segmenting (breaking apart) words into their individual sounds. These skills are necessary for word recognition and spelling.

Children with dyslexia have significant difficulties with phonics. For many of them, learning how to break the code of sound-symbol relationships is an arduous process. Teaching students with dyslexia to read requires the use of research-based methods, which include effective phonics instruction.

What Research Tells Us

- While many first graders are ready to read trade books, students with dyslexia and others with reading weaknesses may need a program that mainly focuses on teaching phonics and word recognition skills. Guided reading lessons (students work in small groups with the teacher to learn reading skills and strategies) in the early education classroom should be accompanied by intensive phonics instruction, especially for students with reading problems.

- Dyslexic students who receive intensive, explicit phonics-based instruction as early as possible are more likely to eventually read at grade level. The longer this type of instruction is delayed, the more difficult it becomes to remedy reading problems.

- Knowledge of phonics has a positive impact on decoding (word reading), comprehension of text, and spelling. Direct instruction in phonics, using multisensory, systematic strategies, is necessary for students with reading disabilities.

- Interventions for children with dyslexia should ideally be delivered in the form of intensive one-on-one work or in small groups, using a systematic, explicit phonics and phonological awareness curriculum.

Explicit, Systematic Phonics Instruction

There are twenty-six letters in the English alphabet, and there are forty-four sounds made by those letters. Once this alphabetic code is learned, children are able to read and write both familiar and unfamiliar words. Explicit, systematic phonics instruction is essential in any program for beginning readers and for students with reading disabilities of any age.

- Systematic phonics means initially teaching just a few consonants and vowels that have regular sound and spelling patterns (for example, –at, -ag, -am words), then building on that base to read and spell all consonants, vowels, and regular and irregular sounds and spellings.

- Explicit instruction means directly teaching phonics with lots of practice and teacher feedback. Students should be assessed frequently in order to monitor their learning.

- Instruction should be matched to students' developmental levels.

- There should be many teacher-student interactions during lessons. Students should be actively involved in the sessions. For example, students can use manipulatives like word tiles to make words or sort words according to long or short vowel sounds.

- Phonics instruction for children with dyslexia should involve multisensory strategies. Children might be asked to trace with their fingers large letters that have been cut out of sandpaper while saying the sound the letter makes. Some programs teach students to pay attention to how their mouth feels when they are saying each sound. Having students write letters on a whiteboard or in wet sand while saying the corresponding sound out loud is another multi-sensory strategy.

- Provide practice in writing words with the letter-sound association just learned in order to reinforce the connection between sound and print.

Phonics Instruction Sequence

When presenting phonics skills, a sequence should be followed. Skills should be frequently reviewed so that students do not lose the information they have already learned.

- For the initial presentation of letter-sound correspondences, introduce letters/sounds in a sequence similar to this one: ă m t s ĭ f d r ŏ g l h ŭ c b n k v ĕ w j p y x q z.

- Introduce high-frequency letter combinations before low-frequency ones (for example, the letters *m, s, t* before letters such as *q, v, z, x* or the digraph *sh* before *ph*).

- Separate letters that look or sound alike (*e/i, b/d, m/n, p/d, d/t, h/n*).

- Initially, introduce only the most common sound for a letter. (For example, the most common sound for the letter *g* is the /g/ sound in *goat*; the less common sound for that letter is /j/ as in *gym*.)

- Teach easier before more difficult correspondences (continuous sounds, such as /f/ and /m/ that can be held and extended as long as you have breath to hold them: (fff, mmm) before stop sounds such as /p/ and /t/, which cannot be held.

- Teach the short vowels before the long vowels. Most well-designed phonics programs introduce one vowel (short *a*) and a few consonants so that reading and writing simple words (for example, *bat, man*) can begin immediately. Then a second short vowel (usually short *i*) is introduced, along with more consonants, until all short vowels have been taught.

- Teach students how to blend letters together to read words.
- Teach beginning and ending blends (for example, *bl-, cr-, -nd, -st*).
- Teach long vowel sounds. Vowels with regular spelling are taught first (*go, hi, me*), then long vowels with the final *e* rule (*made, cute*).
- Teach vowel digraphs (vowel teams) that are regular (*weed, neat, boat*). Regular vowel digraphs follow the rule that the first vowel says its name and the second is silent. Irregular vowel digraphs that do not follow that rule (for example, in *head, rein,* or *field*) should be taught later.
- Introduce students to easy, decodable books that have many words that contain letters/sounds and phonics patterns they have been taught (for example, "The fat rat ran from the black cat.").

Assessing Phonics Skills

A means of measuring a child's phonics skills is to observe his or her ability to decode nonsense words (also called *nonwords* and *pseudo-words*). These are made-up words that follow rules of English spelling but have no meaning. Because a child has never seen these words and the list provides no context clues, performance on these tests is considered to measure how well a reader figures out unfamiliar words by using phonics. Good readers use their skills efficiently, whereas poor readers who have not mastered letter-sound correspondence do not have strategies for sounding out words. There is a strong relationship between ability to decode nonsense words and ability to decode a real word.

Tests That Measure Phonics Skills

- The DIBELS Nonsense Word Fluency (NWF) http://dibels.uoregon.edu/measures/nwf.php
- The Nonsense Word Test by Scholastic www.scholasticred.com/dodea/pdfs/SPED_TR_nonsense
- The Word Attack test on the Woodcock Reading Mastery Test-Revised (WRMT-R) from the Pearson Assessment Group and Woodcock-Johnson III (WJ-III) from Riverside Publishing

Activities to Reinforce Phonics Skills

- Identifying beginning and ending sounds:
  - Have children come up with as many words as they can that begin with a specific sound.
  - Create word walls with words that have the same beginning or ending sound.
  - Before students line up to leave the room, hand out tickets that each have a word written on them. Release all students who have a word that starts like *ball* or ends like *mud*.
- Connecting letters to sounds:
  - Have students draw letters in finger paint or shaving cream as they say the sound of each letter.
  - Hold up cards with a letter (or blend or digraph) on each. Have everyone say the sound out loud. Ask a volunteer to say a word that starts (or ends) with that sound. This provides a quick review of the letters/sounds that were previously taught.
- Distinguishing vowel sounds:
  - Display commercial or handmade posters of the vowel sounds for easy reference.

- Reading words:
  - Teach consonants and vowels in a sequence that allows students to learn enough to begin reading some words.
  - Provide lots of opportunities for children to read decodable text that reinforces letters/sounds that were taught.
  - Introduce poems and short selections that use letters/sounds that students have learned.
  - Have students write the vowels in a word in different colors from consonants, to help students pay special attention to them.
- Using rime:
  - Provide children with a rime and have them build lists of words by adding onsets. For example, "Using the rime -ing, we can write *ring, thing, string*"). Some students call these groups *word families*.
  - Hand out word cards to students. Have them line up behind the other students who have the same rime in their word.
- Building words by blending letters together:
  - Use cards with a different letter on each one, or use magnetic letters and a board. Have children use these letters to build words.
- Using rhyme:
  - Play matching games using word cards. A match consists of two words that rhyme. This activity can be formatted as a card game, a board game, or a bingo game.
- Learning about consonant blends:
  - Hang clotheslines around the room. Use clothespins to hang word cards that begin with the same consonant blend such as *br, gl,* or *str* or that end with a consonant blend such as *st* or *mp*. Students can add their own words, too.

2.3 Decoding Strategies

- *Decoding* is the process of applying word attack strategies to figure out an unknown word. Words are sounded out by reading each sound connected to a letter or letter pattern and then combining those sounds to form a word. There are too many words in our language for children to be able to memorize each word as a means of identifying it in reading. Decoding enables a reader to identify even words never seen before.

- Skilled readers are able to decode quickly and accurately. Being able to decode with automaticity enables a reader to concentrate on the meaning of the vocabulary and the text.

- In first grade, children learn to sound out and blend sounds and are expected to decode one-syllable words with short and long vowel spellings.

- In grades 2–6, children learn to decode multisyllabic words and become familiar with the different syllable types (described later in this checklist).

- In grades 3–6, the focus is on prefixes, suffixes, Greek and Latin roots, and other word parts.

- As students become proficient at sounding out words, they begin using a sight strategy to identify many words. When they read and see what they recognize from past experience, they no longer need to sound out those words. Good readers begin to recognize many words purely by sight, which helps speed up the reading process.

Teaching Decoding Skills

- Decoding instruction begins when children learn beginning phonics. As students master simple skills, more complex word recognition skills are taught. Students who continue to demonstrate weaknesses in decoding may require decoding instruction beyond the elementary grades.

- Once children have learned letter-sound relationships, they learn to decode syllables with regular spelling patterns by blending each of the letters or letter clusters.

- Blending may be an especially difficult process for dyslexic readers. They need explicit instruction in blending skills:

  - Ask students to blend the individual sounds in a one-syllable word without stopping (*fffuunnn*). This is done orally while looking at the letters.

  - Next, have students blend the sounds together quickly (*fun*).

  - As they gain skill, students will begin to decode silently. Have them ask themselves whether each word decoded is a real word and whether it makes sense within the context of what they are reading. If not, they should try decoding the word again.

- Students need to be introduced to vowel spellings that may have different sounds (such as *ou* in *touch* or *cloud*).

- With more experience, children can begin to read familiar chunks as a unit instead of sounding out each letter. They may recognize phonograms (such as *ight* in *sight*) or prefixes (*pre* in *precook*) and suffixes (*ing* in *cooking*).

- Students need to be taught to look carefully inside new words for chunks or small words that they already know, to help them figure out unfamiliar words (*out* in *snout*, *man* in *mansion*).

- Instruction in morphology begins in the middle elementary grades. Morphology involves the study of how morphemes (the smallest unit of meaning in the language, such as prefixes and suffixes) affect the meanings of words.

- In the upper elementary grades, instruction focuses on teaching students strategies to use when they encounter multisyllabic words and English words derived from Greek and Latin roots.

Teaching Decoding to Students with Dyslexia

Students with dyslexia

- Generally have phonological processing weaknesses that cause them significantly more difficulty in decoding and identifying words than their peers have.
- Typically have the cognitive ability to understand vocabulary and comprehend what they read but have difficulty at the more basic level of decoding individual words.
- Need repeated experience in working with decoding skills and concepts using multisensory techniques as well as more intensity of instruction.
- Benefit from decoding instruction that uses a research-based language program. (See Checklist 1.8.)

Approaches to Word Recognition

Students learn different approaches to recognizing words when they read:

- *Decoding:* sounding out letters or letter clusters and blending them together.
- *Analogy:* using another similar word to figure out the new word. (For example, knowing the word *fight* helps a reader figure out the word *sight* or *frighten*.)
- *Context:* using context, as well as language skills or background knowledge, to guess what the word will be, sometimes using the first one or two letters to make the guess. (For example, "The cow gives us m _____.") Experienced readers who have background knowledge about cows will be able to make a good guess that the word is *milk*, without having to even sound out the remainder of the word. If a word does not make sense in the context within which it was read, the student tries decoding the word again.
- *Sight words:* recognizing a word because it has been read before.
- *Chunking:* looking within a word to find a familiar word or chunk (for example, *low* in *below*).

Onset-Rime Blending

Studying onset and rime in words benefits students with reading difficulties. Students can be taught to break syllables into *onset* (everything before the vowel) and *rime* (the vowel and everything after it). Using onset-rime patterns they already know, students are then able to figure out new words. (If you know the word *back*, you can figure out *sn-ack* and *tr-ack*).

There are thirty-seven rimes that can form hundreds of words. Knowing these rimes (also known as *chunks* or *word families*) provides students with important skills for decoding and spelling. Here are some examples of these rimes:

-ack	-aw	-ink
-ain	-ay	-ip
-ake	-eat	-it

Body-Coda Blending

Another approach to blending is to use body and coda. The *body* of a syllable contains all of the phonemes up to and including the vowel. The consonant (or consonants) that come after the vowel are called the *coda*. The word *creep*, separated into body and coda, would be *cree-p*.

Because body-coda blending places emphasis on the vowel, a student may find it easier to stretch out the vowel when reading it aloud. For some children, it is easier to do body-coda blending because there is less sound distortion when the body is read and then blended with the coda than when onset and rime are blended.

A syllable, then, can be divided on either side of the vowel. The word *flat* can be broken up in two ways: onset-rime (fl-at) or body-coda (fla-t).

Assessing Word Identification Skills Using Miscue Analysis

- *Miscue analysis* is a system used to examine a student's skills in word recognition by listening to the student read aloud from selected passages. Rather than have students read from a list of words, this provides a look at how a child reads in context.

- As a child reads aloud, teachers look at the errors (miscues) that are made in order to try to understand how a student identifies words as he or she reads. Teachers examine misread words for clues about how a child approaches word identification.

- Students use different kind of cues to identify a word:
  - *Letter-sound cues:* sounding out the word. If a student consistently sounds out letters incorrectly, this serves as an indication that those letter-sounds have not yet been mastered.
  - *Context cues:* using a word that fits in the meaning of the sentence. A miscue might be reading "The boy saw his *mom*" when the word is actually *mother*.
  - *Syntax:* using sentence structure, grammar, word order. In the sentence "He is g _____ on a trip," the word *going* would fit in the blank, but the word *go* would not.

- Weak readers rely on context when they have poor word recognition skills, but this is inadequate when the material becomes more difficult. When teachers evaluate the reading of older readers, they look for miscues that indicate that a reader has become overly reliant on context clues, and is doing insufficient word decoding work. A child who reads the sentence, "The bear ran to its cave" as "The bear ran to its cage" has made this kind of error. These types of miscues have an impact on comprehension as reading material becomes more complex. The sentence, "He gave her pears" has a much different meaning than "He gave her pearls."

- Informal reading inventories and running records are used to estimate a student's instructional and independent reading levels. Running records are used by teachers to see how a student reads. As a child reads orally from a selected piece of text, the teacher takes notes on errors, hesitations, self-corrections, and substitutions made by the reader.

- Informal reading inventories are commercially available or teacher-prepared collections of passages at different grade levels. Students are tested on fluency and comprehension skills in order to identify their appropriate independent reading level.

Activities for Teaching Decoding

- Use spinners, dominoes, or cards. Create some cards or dominoes with onsets and others with rimes. Students match rimes with an onset to create words. Have students work together to build as many words as they can from a given rime such as with -ink: pink, think, stink.
- Use word sorts. By sorting words, students have the opportunity to look closely at them to figure out similarities and differences.
  - Word sort activities provide students with the opportunity to sort words by rimes (-ane and –ain), in order to focus on the various spellings of a single rime or to differentiate words by identifying words that rhyme with each other. (The word cards name and tame would be placed under same; ham and ram would be placed under jam.) Students sort a series of cards (at their desk or on the floor) by putting them under the correct heading placed at the top of each category column.
  - Word sorts can be used to provide practice in decoding skills. For example, students can be asked to find words with silent letters (such as knock), words that follow the silent e rule (make and bike), words that share common vowel sounds, or words that have a common beginning sound.
- Use decodable texts (books that contain words with letter-sound patterns that are familiar to students) as part of early

reading instruction. Students can use their newly developed word recognition skills to read books independently.

- Use high-interest books with easy vocabulary for older students with weak word recognition skills.

- Use parent volunteers and peer tutors to provide students with increased reading practice.

- Create word walls or individual pages in a bound notebook. Each wall or page will contain one word chunk or word family such as *-eat, -ill, -un*. Have students add words that contain a particular chunk to each wall or page.

- Provide students with horizontal rows of words, each containing several similar-looking words (for example, *her, hair, here*). For each row, call out one of the words and have students circle it. This activity requires students to look carefully at the "insides" of words.

Syllables and Word Parts: The Key to Unlocking Big Words

Multisyllabic words—"big words" with two or more syllables—can pose a challenge to students with dyslexia. It is particularly important to teach dyslexic readers that they can learn strategies to segment long words, breaking them into smaller, more manageable chunks. Older students who have weak word recognition and spelling skills need considerable work at this level—learning about word parts and strategies for unlocking big words.

Learning About Syllables

Young children begin to learn about syllables when they stretch out words and practice counting, clapping, or tapping out syllables in words they hear, such as their name. This is a key phonological awareness skill. For example, "Clap the syllables you hear in 'rabbit' (two claps), 'elephant' (three claps)." (See Checklist 2.1.)

When they are developmentally ready, children should be taught that

- A syllable is a word part that can be said in one breath.
- Every syllable includes a vowel. (Sometimes y is a vowel.)
- The vowel sounds can be spelled in various ways: a single letter (*a, e, i, o, u, y*); double vowels like *ai, ee, ou;* and other combinations (for example, *r*-controlled: *ar, or, ur*).
- Sometimes a vowel that is written in the syllable is silent (such as the *e* in *cake* or *bot-tle*).
- There are six types of syllables. Knowing the syllable types will help students figure out vowel sounds and how to read and spell words that contain those letter patterns.

The Six Types of Syllables

The English language is made up of the following syllable types:

1. *Closed syllables* have only one vowel followed by one or more consonants. The vowel is closed in by the ending consonant or consonants. The vowel almost always makes the short sound (*mŏp, făst, pĭc/nĭc, căc/tŭs*).

2. *Open syllables* end with a single vowel. The vowel has nothing following it or closing it in. The vowel sound is usually long ("says its name"), as in *bē, tū/lip, hō/tel, ī/dol*.

3. *Vowel-consonant-e syllables* are also called *final e* or *magic e syllables*. In this syllable, a vowel is followed by one consonant and the letter *e*. The first vowel is long ("says its name") and the *e* at the end is silent, as in *cāke, rep/tīle, tad/pōle*.

4. *R-controlled syllables* have a vowel followed by the letter *r* (*ar, or, ir, er, ur*). The vowel sound is controlled by the *r* and makes a different vowel sound—neither short nor long. Examples include the sounds heard in *ar* words (*farm, mar/ket*), *or* words (*cork, for/tress*), and *er, ir,* and *ur* words (*birth, fur/ther*).

5. *Vowel team* or *double vowel syllables* have two consecutive vowels. Usually, the first vowel in the team makes a long

sound and the second is silent, following the rule that "When two vowels go walking, the first does the talking," as in *hēat*, *re/māin*, and *un/lōad*. Less frequently, vowel teams make the short-vowel sound, as in *brĕad*. Other double vowel combinations make a different vowel sound, as in diphthongs (*co͜in*, or *bo͜ot*).

6. *Consonant -le syllables* come at the end of a word with a consonant followed by the letters *le*, as in *bun/dle*, *daz/zle*.

Strategies for Chunking and Breaking Apart Words by Syllables

One method for breaking words into manageable chunks is dividing them into syllables through rules of syllabication, then noting the positions of the consonants and vowels in order to determine whether the vowel sounds are long or short.

The two main syllabication rules to teach students are these:

1. When there are two consonants between two vowels (VCCV), the syllables are usually divided between the two consonants (VC-CV). Thus, the first syllable is closed and has a short vowel. Examples: nap-kin and ham-mer. *Note:* Consonant digraphs (for example, *sh*, *th*, and *ch*) are not separated, because they represent a single sound. For example, dash-ing instead of das-hing and go-pher not gop-her.

2. When one consonant comes between two vowels (VCV), the syllables will be divided after the first vowel, before the consonant (V-CV), which will make the first syllable an open syllable with a long vowel sound. Examples: mū-sic, rō-bot. If the word doesn't sound right with that pronunciation, the division would be made after the consonant, as in sev-en and cab-in.

Reading Syllables and Blending Them into Words

- After students divide words into syllables, have them say the vowel sound (according to the syllable type).

- Have students cover all of the word except the first syllable, and then read just the exposed first syllable. Then have them uncover the next word part, and then the next, until they have read all the parts. Next, have them blend all the parts together quickly to read the whole word.

- Provide modeling in segmenting, then blending the word parts into recognizable words, changing the pronunciation if it doesn't sound right. Changing the pronunciation often requires changing the syllable that is accented or stressed (said louder). For example, in reading the word *prefer*, if the child reads it with the first syllable accented (pre´fer) and it doesn't sound familiar, the accent can be changed to the second syllable (pre fer´).

- Provide practice in reading syllables of various types. Make cards with different syllables on them. Students can have drills or flash-card practice with the cards. Some cards might have real one-syllable words (for example, *pile, hard*), or nonsense words (for example, *shile, fomp*). Others might have syllables such as *lo* or *na* that are not words but are part of a multisyllabic word (for example, *lo-cate, na-ture*).

- Have students practice reading multisyllabic words in isolation, in phrases, and in connected sentences. For example, have students read *opinion* (isolation), *in my opinion* (phrase), and *What is your opinion about this book?* (sentence).

Teaching Prefixes, Suffixes, and Other Word Parts

Another important strategy for helping students unlock big words is explicitly teaching them to recognize chunks of words and then to break long words into those parts and blend them back together quickly. Such chunks might include

- Smaller words within a big word (for instance, a compound word) such as *snowboard*.
- Word parts at the beginning or end of a base word (*prefixes* and *suffixes*), which often change the meaning of a base word

or the way a word is used in a sentence. According to Archer, Gleason, and Vachon (2000), approximately 80 percent of multisyllabic words contain one or more prefixes or suffixes.

Prefixes, Suffixes, and Bases

- *Prefix:* a letter or combination of letters that are located in front of base words and that change the meaning of the base word. In the word *disapprove*, *dis* is the prefix. Examples of prefixes and their meanings include *un-* (not), *mis-* (wrong), and *inter-* (between).

- *Base word* (also called *root word*): the main word, to which prefixes and suffixes are added. In the word *unacceptable*, the base word is *accept*.

- *Suffix:* a letter or group of letters that come after the base word and change the meaning of the word (for example, use*ful*, use*less*) or the way the word is used. Examples of suffixes include *-ly*, *-y*, *-ness*, *-ity*. Suffixes often change the part of speech of the base word—for example, *sleep*, *sleeps*, *sleepy*.

Greek and Latin Roots

- Many multisyllabic English words have Greek, Latin, or Anglo-Saxon roots, or bases. For example, *phon* is the Greek root meaning "sound." From that root, many words can be derived—for example, *phonology*, *telephone*, *phonics*. The Latin root *tain* means "to hold." From that root come the words *container* (something that holds things together), *detain* (to hold someone back from going), *abstain* (to hold yourself back or keep away from something).

- Recognizing words with the same root helps students decode long words and understand their meanings.

Strategies for Breaking Apart Words with Prefixes and Suffixes

- Prefixes and suffixes usually are chunked as separate syllables.

- The program REWARDS (Archer, Gleason, & Vachon, 2000) teaches students the following strategy for decoding multisyllabic words:
  1. Circle the prefixes at the beginning of the word and the suffixes at the end.
  2. Underline the letters for vowel sounds in the rest of the word.
  3. Say the parts of the word.
  4. Say the parts fast.
  5. Make it a real word.
- Later, students can be taught to spot the word parts and use the preceding strategy without actually circling or underlining parts of multisyllabic words.

Word Study Activities for Practicing Big Words

Many strategies and activities can help students build skills and practice with syllable types and word parts:

- Write multisyllabic words on strips of paper, divide them into syllables and cut the syllables apart, then have students put them back together and read them.
- Use manipulative letters to change open syllables into closed syllables (*be/beg, hi/hit*) or CVC words into CVCe words (*hop/hope, rat/rate*)
- Make syllable cards that can be moved around to form real words. For example, given four cards: *sect, per, in,* and *son,* students could make the words *insect* and *person.*
- Do word sorts according to word parts or syllable types. Have students work with sets of cards that can be sorted and categorized under two or three headings. For example, cards could be sorted into suffixes (for example, *-er, -est*) and prefixes (for example, *re-, dis-*) or into open and closed syllables.

- After students sort words, have them record the words in categories in a word study notebook.

- Have students create word webs. The root or base word (for example, *satisfy*) would be written in the center of the page. Radiating from that center word like strands of a spider web would be related words such as *satisfies, satisfying, satisfaction, satisfactory, dissatisfied*.

- Ask students to analyze new words in content areas such as social studies and science by identifying and discussing prefixes. (For example, what was the *transcontinental* railroad? What other words do you know that begin like *photosynthesis?*)

2.4 Sight Word and Irregular Word Strategies

As readers become more proficient, they are able to recognize words by sight, rather than decoding each word they see. The larger a reader's sight vocabulary, the easier it becomes to read pages full of words. Improving children's immediate recognition of sight words, as well as irregular words, helps improve overall reading fluency and comprehension.

Sight Words

- When children recognize words by sight, they are able to look at a word as a whole rather than by decoding it sound by sound. If a word is part of a child's sight vocabulary, as soon as it is seen, it is recognized and read. By continual exposure to frequently used words, children are increasingly able to recognize these words with automaticity. Having good decoding skills enables readers to attack many words; having a good store of sight words gives them the ability to read more words on the page quickly and easily.

- Frequent review of sight words is necessary for children to commit them to memory. Sight words should be introduced in early first grade, so that students can begin to read easy books containing both decodable and sight words.

- Students are introduced to sight words early in the reading process because those words are needed to read even simple text. Sight words also become part of a child's spelling knowledge. Being able to spell sight words contributes to greater fluency and accuracy in writing.

- Sight words are words used most often in reading in the English language. The Fry list of the 600 most frequently used words in books and the Dolch list of the 220 most frequent words (not including nouns) are popular references for words that readers should learn.

- Sight words include some that have regular spellings (for example, *go*, *that*), as well as some that have irregular spellings and cannot be decoded according to the usual rules (*said*, *who*, *one*).

- Because dyslexic readers often read less, they may have less exposure to print and therefore may have a smaller number of sight words in their repertoire. By using multisensory techniques and providing repeated exposure to these important words, teachers and parents can help weak readers improve their recognition of sight words.

Irregular Words

- English is full of irregular words (words that do not follow predictable patterns) such as *been*, *does*, and *school* that need to be learned by sight rather than sounded out phonetically.

- By fourth grade, students have been exposed to many irregular words in their reading. Students with dyslexia need additional work through multisensory instruction, drills, and repeated exposure in order to learn as many of these irregular words as possible. If they do not learn common irregular words, their reading fluency becomes further compromised as unsuccessful efforts are made to sound out irregular words according to previously taught rules.

Activities to Help Students Learn Sight Words

- When introducing new sight words, focus on just a few each week.

- Have students think of chants, rhymes, or other auditory techniques to help them remember the spelling of some sight words. For example, students might chant by spelling the word and then saying the whole word: "S . . a . . i . . d, s . . a . . i . . d, said, said."

- Create two sets of cards, each with the same sight words. Students can use the cards to play games like Concentration (turn over two cards; try to find a match), Go Fish, or bingo. The more students see and work with sight words, the more familiar the words become.

- Display sight words prominently on word walls around the room. Word walls can be updated as words are introduced.

- Use newly introduced sight words on the board and in daily schedules, reminders, class messages, and individual notes to students.

- Create word cards that have sight words written with textured material (sandpaper, pasta, pipe cleaners) so that children can feel the words, read them, and say them aloud.

- Use word banks. Each student might have a box like those used for recipes, filled with cards, each containing a sight word. All the words that have been successfully read are placed in one section. Words that are new or have not yet been mastered are placed in a second section (or a second box). The child builds a collection of sight words during the year. Large metal rings that contain hole-punched cards can also be used. They are easy to carry and can be taken on car trips or used during independent work time.

- Use sight words that children are learning as part of the week's spelling list.

- Write group poems that focus on some of the sight words, so that repetition of the words is done in a fun way.

> My dog *is* small.
>
> My dad *is* tall.
>
> And that *is* all.

- Provide students with easy word searches that have embedded sight words.

- Have students complete unfinished sentences with sight words from a list of words provided.

- Ask students to construct their own sentences, using as many sight words as they can. (Provide a list for reference.)

- Teach new irregular words by comparing them with similar words—for example, *is/his, bought/brought/fought.*

- Encourage students to look at irregular words to see what makes them tricky. (For example, in *ghost,* the *h* is silent; in the word *were,* the *e* at the end is silent.) Have students come up with their own ideas for ways to remember the words. Students can use highlighters to identify the part of the word they find unusual—for example, the *w* in *two* or the *gh* in *though.*

- Preview new words that students will encounter in their reading in content areas such as social studies and science. These might include words that have spelling irregularities or that are derived from another language— for example, *island, Sioux.* Attempts at decoding those words will not work, and may add to a poor reader's frustration.

Sight Word Lists

- **Dolch word list:** E. W. Dolch created a list of 220 words (not including nouns) that are found most frequently in books. These words make up 50–75 percent of the words that students read. The following Web sites contain the Dolch word list and related activities:

  www.quiz-tree.com/

  www.theschoolbell.com

  www.learningbooks.net.

  www.dolchsightwords.org/

- **Fry's Instant Words:** This list of words in order of frequency of use was developed by Edward Fry. The list is available at the following sites:

    http://www.uen.org/k-2educator/word_lists.shtml#frywords

    http://www.usu.edu/teachall/text/reading/Frylist.pdf

    The list is also available in *The Reading Teacher's Book of Lists* (Fry & Kress, 2006).

2.5 Fluency Strategies

Fluency is the ability to read effortlessly with accuracy, automaticity, speed, and expression. Research shows that fluency is
directly correlated to comprehension.

Fluency is a significant weakness for readers with dyslexia,
whose reading is often very slow, labored, and lacking in expression, which in turn affects reading comprehension.

Factors That Contribute to Fluency

- *Accuracy:* being able to decode or recognize words correctly.
  Building phonics skills, word attack skills, and sight recognition of high-frequency and irregular words is necessary to
  improve reading accuracy.

- *Rate:* being able to read individual words and connected text
  quickly. Reading speed (rate) increases with practice and
  re-reading. Rate is measured by words correct per minute or
  length of time needed to complete a passage.

- *Automaticity:* accurate, effortless, and rapid word recognition—not having to put mental effort into identifying
  words. Automaticity requires rapid decoding of unfamiliar
  words and recognizing a high number of familiar words
  by sight. Practice and memory play a significant part in
  automaticity.

- *Prosody:* being able to read with good expression that
  sounds like speech (appropriate pitch, tone, phrasing, stress
  or emphasis, pacing, and rhythm). Prosody, which plays
  an important part in comprehension of text, is developed
  through listening to good reading models and practice.

- *Vocabulary:* word knowledge. Knowing the meaning of a
  word makes it easier and quicker to read. Vocabulary development increases fluency by improving recognition of words
  in print.

- *Processing speed:* how quickly one processes information—for example, on seeing written words, how quickly one can convert those symbols into speech (whether one is reading silently or aloud).

- *Reading volume:* how much one reads. The more children read, the greater their exposure to words will be, facilitating vocabulary acquisition and word recognition. Struggling readers read less because it is not pleasurable; therefore, they often get less exposure to words and less practice than their grade-level peers.

- *Correct practice:* repeated use of reading skills. Fluency is developed through many opportunities to practice skills correctly, which means reading aloud to an adult or skilled reader who can provide corrective feedback as needed.

Research-Based Strategies for Building Fluency

Research shows that fluency can be developed through a variety of techniques, particularly through repeated monitored oral reading.

Repeated Oral Reading: Re-Reading Strategies for Fluency

- *Student-adult reading.* The adult reads aloud first, providing a model of fluent reading. The student then re-reads the same passage, with adult assistance and coaching as needed. For example, if the student gets stuck on a word, the adult reads the word and the child repeats it. The student re-reads the passage a few times until it is read fluently with ease and expression.

- *Partner reading, or buddy reading.* Partner reading can be done in various ways. One way is to pair a stronger reader with a less fluent reader. The stronger reader first reads the page or passage aloud, pointing to the words while the partner follows along. Then, the less fluent reader re-reads the same passage while the stronger partner assists and coaches (gently correcting errors, after which the partner re-reads the passage). In another variation, partners at the same reading level are paired in order to re-read a passage or story a few times in different formats—for example,

- Alternating paragraphs or pages
- Having first one partner read the whole passage, then the other
- Having one partner read for a few minutes, then switching
- Reading in unison while one person points under the words

- *Choral reading*. This technique involves reading text aloud in unison after it is first modeled for fluent oral reading. Everyone looks at the text as it is read. There are different ways of doing choral reading in the classroom: using individual copies for re-reading aloud together, or providing large-size text that students can see from where they are seated. This is usually done by projecting text on a screen via an overhead projector or document camera using a "big book," or writing the words of a poem, song, or passage in large print on the board or chart paper.
  - The teacher models and reads the text with fluency while sweeping a finger or marker under the words in phrases—not word by word—to match the flow of speech.
  - The material is re-read; this time, students join in for choral re-reading of all or parts of the text a few times.
  - For fun, teachers can vary sections of the text to be read by different groups (for example, boys and girls, left side of room and right side of room).

- *Echo reading*. The teacher reads aloud a short section of text (a single sentence, a paragraph, or a verse of a poem).

Immediately, the students echo what was just read while the teacher points to or sweeps under the words. Echo reading can be done with a whole group or just an individual student. Poetry and song lyrics work well for fluency practice.

- *Recording-assisted reading.* A student reads along with a passage or book on CD recorded by a fluent reader. After hearing it read several times, the student reads along with the recording and practices until the text can be read fluently. Some recorded books may not be appropriate for fluency practice because they may have too many unfamiliar words or concepts.

- *Software programs.* Students use a program such as Read Naturally (www.readnaturally.com), which combines teacher modeling, repeated reading, assessment, and progress monitoring on the computer.

- *Readers theater.* Many theater scripts are excellent for fluency practice. Students practice reading their assigned parts from the script in order to perform for classmates or other audiences.

- *Practicing in order to perform.* In addition to readers theater, many other performance opportunities—for example, puppet shows, plays, choral concerts, or poetry parties—can provide a means of getting struggling readers to practice fluency by rehearsing in preparation for performance.

- *Cross-age buddy reading.* Older students often have younger reading buddies. Reading a book with good expression provides fluency practice in preparation for reading that book to their younger buddy.

- *Timed repeated reading and charting.* Students read a short passage for one minute. The teacher determines the words correct per minute (reading rate) on that passage, and the student charts or graphs the score. This procedure continues with repeated readings until the target reading rate is reached.

Other Fluency-Building Strategies

- For fluency of letter/sound and word recognition, use flash card drills (timed or untimed) to increase speed and automaticity. This technique works for quick naming of letters and sound associations, phonics patterns (such as -ow, -ing, -ide), and irregular and high-frequency sight words and phrases. For practice at this level (single words, parts of words), game formats are the most motivating. Students may race against themselves.

- Teach students to read text in phrases, not word by word. For example, "The little girl / ran to the door / when her dad came home." When you are having students repeat phrases, sweep under the phrase instead of each word.

- Read aloud frequently; modeling fluent, expressive reading of various genres of text is very important in the development of children's word knowledge, comprehension, and fluency.

- Motivate children to read in and out of school. At-risk readers need to increase their reading volume significantly for adequate practice. Providing high-interest selections at the appropriate level is key to increasing reading volume by motivating reluctant readers to *choose* to read and practice.

- In fluency practice for connected text (reading not isolated words but passages, poems, or other material), emphasize reading for comprehension, not speed. That means smooth reading with appropriate speed, phrasing, and expression so that the text makes sense.

- Be sure the reader is practicing correctly—reading words accurately, with assistance provided as needed.

- Provide prompts when listening to a child read orally. Say, for example, "Pause when you see a comma." "Read that part again quickly." "Notice the exclamation mark."

The Challenge of Remediating

- For older students with reading disabilities, fluency is probably the most difficult area to remediate because of the cumulative effect of years of minimal practice in reading words correctly.

- Lack of correct practice results in a huge deficiency in the number of words that the reader can recognize instantly by sight and a much slower reading rate than grade-level peers.

Fluency-Building Programs

- Jamestown Timed Readings by Glencoe, McGraw-Hill, are passages of varying reading levels for the purpose of increasing the reading rate and fluency of adolescents. www.glencoe.com

- Quick Reads®, by Text Project, foster development of oral reading skills through practice of reading one-minute informational text passages in print or on the computer. www.quickreads.org (See Checklist 1.8.)

- Read Naturally is a well-researched intervention program combining teacher modeling, repeated reading, assessment, and progress monitoring. www.readnaturally.com (See Checklist 1.8.)

- The Fluency Formula™ Program, by Scholastic, is a supplemental program for readers in grades 1–6. www.scholastic.com

Assessing Fluency

According to the U.S. National Reading Panel, fluency is a predictor of reading success. It is now common practice for elementary schools to perform oral reading fluency assessments a few times a year to identify students in need of intervention and to measure students' progress.

- Fluency assessments generally measure rate and accuracy, using one-minute readings from an unpracticed passage that is appropriate for the reader's grade level.

- The teacher listens to the student read the passage aloud for one minute and subtracts each error from the total words read in order to determine the words correct per minute, which is compared with grade-level norms for that time of the school year.

- Quick fluency assessments for screening purposes have been proven as valid, reliable indicators of general reading achievement for most students.

- Some fluency assessments include the Dynamic Indicators of Basic Early Literacy Skills (DIBELS) Oral Reading Fluency Probes (http://dibels.uoregon.edu) and AimsWeb (http://edformation.com).

- Norm charts include the National Oral Reading Fluency norms for grades 1–8 (Hasbrouck and Tindal, 2005) and those that come with specific fluency programs such as Read Naturally (www.readnaturally.com) and The Fluency Formula™ (www.scholastic.com).

2.6 Vocabulary Strategies

Knowledge of vocabulary or word meanings has been identified as a key factor in reading success. The more words a person knows, the better he or she is able to comprehend and communicate in speaking, reading, and writing. Word knowledge affects understanding of concepts in all content areas. All subject areas require mastery of specific vocabulary terms, so students with a weak vocabulary are at a significant disadvantage in school.

Although many students with dyslexia have a strong oral vocabulary, their poor reading skills impede their recognition and acquisition of the hundreds of new words that their classmates who are skilled readers learn through reading. Students who read a lot are exposed to complicated, sophisticated words through their reading and have a stronger vocabulary than minimal readers.

Additional Problems for Dyslexics

- Poor language processing and poor retrieval of words from memory restrict word usage when speaking and writing (oral and written vocabulary).
- Deficient word knowledge affects general knowledge and expression of ideas.
- Underlying language difficulties impede comprehension of words with multiple meanings (such as *tear, trunk,* or *punch*) and figures of speech (metaphors, idioms, puns).
- As children read more difficult books, exposure to complex vocabulary is increased. A child with a reading disability is less able to independently read vocabulary-rich books, reducing exposure to high-level vocabulary.

Developing Vocabulary

Many new words are learned indirectly through listening or seeing words used in context. However, in order for students to acquire mastery of all the words they need for academic success, many words need to be taught directly. Vocabulary research has identified these approaches as the best ways to develop students' vocabulary:

- Encourage children to read widely from literature as well as informational text.
- Provide multiple exposures and opportunities to see, hear, and use newly learned words.
- Link new words to students' background knowledge and experiences.
- Provide direct instruction in word learning strategies to enable students to figure out meaning of unknown words on their own. Word learning strategies include making use of context clues (the sentence containing the unknown word and surrounding sentences), knowledge of word parts (prefixes, suffixes, roots), and looking up definitions.
- Engage children in conversations and oral language activities.
- Read to children from books that have rich language—paraphrasing and explaining new vocabulary words.
- Engage students in strategies to *actively* process and work with new words in multiple ways.
- Preview text and explain important words prior to reading so students can watch for those words while they are reading.
- Explicitly teach strategies for developing memory cues, links, and associations for new words.
- Foster word consciousness—awareness and appreciation of the power of words.
- Use student-friendly language that is concise to explain word meanings and word usage.
- Show illustrations or other images to support explanations of word meanings.

- Teach dictionary and thesaurus skills.
- Review vocabulary words, and check for comprehension and retention of new words.

Strategies for Vocabulary Instruction and Working with Words

- *Directly teaching words:* Define words for students using simple explanations and synonyms. If possible, use antonyms (opposites) as well. For example, tell students, "The word *emaciated* means really skinny—extremely thin, often from starving. It's the opposite of fat or plump." *Give examples and non-examples:* "The starving kitten was weak and emaciated when they found it." "Might a child living in poverty who is undernourished be emaciated?" "Do these people look emaciated?" (Show pictures of average and heavy people.) Have students *generate their own examples* of the word in a sentence or with a picture.

- *Context clues:* Reading a word in the context of the rest of the sentence and surrounding sentences is an important strategy for figuring out meanings of unknown words. Have students read a word (or listen to it being read) in the context of the surrounding sentences and try to guess the meaning.

- *Cloze technique:* This is a strategy for using surrounding words to figure out a missing word. It is a fill-in-the-blank activity in which the student makes use of context clues to determine the missing words. Take a short piece of text and delete some of the words, replacing each word with a blank line (_____). Have students read the passage and fill in the blanks. (You may want to provide a word bank.) After students have completed the activity, discuss the words that were chosen.

- *Semantic webs:* These are visual displays or graphic organizers for helping students learn vocabulary and understand word relationships. Write a specific vocabulary word in the center of the page. Other related words, phrases, characteristics, properties, or examples relating to that word are written around the page, radiating from the center vocabulary word (like a spider web).

- *Multiple meanings:* Provide practice in working with words with multiple meanings. *Homophones* (also called *homonyms*) are words that sound the same but have different meanings. Homophones include words that are spelled and pronounced the same but are different in meaning, such as *bark* (which could mean a dog's bark or the bark of tree). Homophones also include words that are pronounced the same but have different meanings and spellings—for example, *week/weak, to/too/two*. Have students perform activities in which they identify, categorize, match, list, and make up riddles with homophones.

- *Word parts:* Teach students to recognize and divide words into their meaningful parts (morphemes). Morphemes include *prefixes, suffixes,* and *roots* (or *bases*). Provide practice and activities that engage students in learning about morphemes in order to figure out the meanings of words based on those parts—for example, *bi-month-ly* (twice a month), *in-flex-ible* (not able to flex or bend). Teach students how adding prefixes and suffixes changes the meanings of words.

- *Word lists or charts:* Post lists of words, adding to them throughout the year as new words are encountered. Topics for these lists might include

  - Character traits—for example, *inquisitive, stubborn, compassionate.*

  - Feelings—for example, *suspicious, optimistic, discouraged.*

  - Alternatives to overused words such as *said, went,* or *nice*—for example, alternatives to *said* might include *stated, responded, announced.*

- *Definitions:* Teach dictionary skills. Model and provide practice in looking up words in references such as a dictionary, glossary, or thesaurus.

- *Make it visual, make it memorable.* Make illustrations, use symbols to represent ideas, label, color, highlight, or use graphic organizers to help students remember words and their associations with other words or ideas.

- *Games and word play:* Games that build vocabulary and make learning about words fun can be made or purchased. Word games can be frustrating for children with dyslexia, particularly if they require speed in reading or word retrieval. Choose games carefully, or make adaptations as needed (extended or no time limits, providing assistance in reading words on the game card).

  - Use age-appropriate crossword puzzles.

  - Play commercial games that enhance vocabulary and language skills, such as Password, Jeopardy, One Minute Wonders, Outburst, and Pictionary.

  - Share riddles, and have students make up their own.

- *Mapping unknown words:* Provide activities that require students to map information for a new word. Have them write the word and sentence in which it is found in the text; record its definition, synonyms for the word, and an example or illustration; and write a sentence using the word.

- *Figurative language:* Students with language processing disorders often have difficulty with understanding figures of speech and nuances of language such as idioms, puns, and metaphors. Teach these elements through a variety of activities:

  - Share idioms such as "He saw the handwriting on the wall." Explain the difference between literal and figurative meaning. Have students make a drawing of both, such as a man staring at a wall with handwriting scrawled

STRATEGIES FOR HELPING   103

all over it (literal) and a man about to be pulled over for a ticket for speeding through a red light (figurative).

- Find examples of metaphors to chart and illustrate. Examples: "The man is a rock." "That is a half-baked idea."

- *Precision with words:* Teach students how valuable it is to use just the right words to convey meaning most precisely. Provide activities in which students work in groups or partners to arrange an array of words along a continuum—for example, words that describe moving from here to there: *ambled . . . strolled . . . walked . . . jogged . . . dashed.*

- See the vocabulary resources at the end of this section, which provide Web sites for online dictionaries, thesauri, word games, and vocabulary-building activities.

2.7 Comprehension Strategies

Comprehension—getting meaning from text—is the purpose of reading. Comprehension is influenced by factors such as word recognition, fluency, vocabulary, background knowledge, information processing, memory, awareness of text structure, and reading experience. Reading comprehension requires the reader to *actively process* the text, self-monitor for understanding, and know how and when to apply various meaning-making strategies when something doesn't make sense.

Students with reading disabilities need explicit comprehension instruction in order to learn effective strategies and how to implement them in independent reading.

Strategies That Good Readers Use

For students with reading disabilities, the processes and strategies that good readers use must be taught and practiced extensively. Good readers

- Make connections to other books that they have previously read (text to text), to their own life and experiences (text to self), and to other information they know (text to world).
- Use metacognition—awareness of their thinking and understanding. Students self-monitor and self-regulate while reading—that is, they recognize when they do not understand something and apply strategies in order to solve problems.
- Apply self-correction strategies when they are confused about what they read.
- Constantly predict and confirm or change predictions as they read.
- Understand the organization and structure of different types of text: literary (narrative) and informational (expository).
- Visualize while reading, making mental images (mind movies).

- Distinguish main ideas and important information from details and less important information.

- Engage in many kinds of critical thinking processes—for example, reflecting, questioning, and evaluating—while reading.

- Determine which strategies to use and when, depending on the reading task and type of material. For example, they know how to skim through a textbook chapter (expository text), looking at the headings, subheadings, and graphics in order to get an overview of the content before reading, and they know when it is important to understand the meaning of all the words (test instructions) and when it is not necessary (a magazine ad).

Why Dyslexic Readers May Have Comprehension Problems

One major problem for students with dyslexia is that textbooks and other reading material for their grade level may be written at a level that exceeds their independent reading ability, making it difficult for them to figure out words and understand vocabulary, which affects their ability to derive meaning from the text.

Students with dyslexia may have trouble with reading comprehension for many reasons:

- Less prior knowledge and vocabulary in content areas as a result of significantly less reading experience or being confused when the material is discussed in class

- Lack of awareness of text structure (for example, elements of story structure, genre differences, organization of informational text)

- Difficulty in remembering (short and long term) what was read or sequence of events and information

- Difficulty in sifting out important information from less relevant information
- Poor metacognitive skills—unaware of their thinking processes, unable to self-monitor or apply strategies
- Slow, laborious reading, making it harder to hold on to meaning

Factors to Consider in Teaching Students with Dyslexia

- Students with dyslexia generally have the ability to comprehend at an average to advanced level when material is heard (good listening comprehension). Provide opportunities for listening to the text being read by a fluent reader.
- Providing accommodations (such as buddy reading) and assistive technology (such as recorded books or text-to-speech software) enable students with reading disabilities to access grade-level and advanced material. (See Checklist 2.13.)
- Students with dyslexia may experience embarrassment when they must read books that are different from those of their peers, particularly if the materials are perceived as babyish. Sensitivity to this issue, as well as finding appropriate material for independent reading, are very important.

Instructional Requirements for Dyslexic Students

Key factors in teaching comprehension skills and strategies to all students, but with more intensity and corrective feedback for students with reading disabilities, include these:

- Be explicit. Tell students directly what the strategies are and how they are beneficial.

- Model the use of strategies that are being taught. Model strategies such as stopping to make predictions, asking yourself questions, describing what is visualized, working through problems to figure out unknown vocabulary, or making connections.
- Provide extensive guided practice in which students use the strategy with teacher support.
- Provide opportunities for students to apply strategies independently or through collaboration with others (in a small group or with a partner).
- Teach multiple research-based strategies, methods, and approaches (such as those described in the remainder of this checklist). There is no one best way that works for everyone.

Strategies for Monitoring Comprehension

Metacognition is an essential brain process that is often developmentally immature in children with dyslexia. Metacognition is the ability to think about one's thinking and self-regulate accordingly. It involves self-awareness, self-monitoring, and being strategic in solving problems. It is important to teach students to monitor their comprehension so that they are aware of what they do and do not understand. Research supports the use of these strategies for monitoring comprehension:

- *K-W-L.* This strategy begins prior to reading but continues during and after the process. Use a chart divided into three columns:
  - The first column (K) indicates what is already *known* about the subject. This step activates students' prior knowledge. Ideas are recorded during a class brainstorming session.

- The middle column (W) is *what* students want to learn or discover about the subject, which sets the purpose for reading.
- The third column indicates what was *learned* (L) and is filled in during or after new information is learned from the reading or other teaching.

- *Summarizing.* This skill is one of the most important in reading comprehension. Summarizing involves identifying the main idea, which sometimes is explicit and easy to find and other times is implied or embedded in the passage. Summarizing techniques require students to stop at points in the reading to paraphrase or summarize. Students can summarize by

  - Responding verbally—for example, telling their reading partner in one sentence what the paragraph was about

  - Filling out graphic organizers with one or two lines for key information

  - Writing a summary sentence or paragraph

  - Composing a heading or title for the passage

  - Identifying who or what the passage is about and what the big idea is for that who or what

- *Reading logs.* Students write feelings, connections, and questions in response to the reading. They may be given prompts to guide them: "What did you learn?" "How does this story relate to your life experiences?"

- *Double-entry journal.* The paper is divided into two columns. Notes are taken in the left column, citing anything of particular interest—such as quotes, descriptions, or metaphors—along with the page number. In the right-hand column, the reader comments and records personal thoughts, connections, and questions triggered by that section of the text.

Comprehension Strategies for Use Before, During, and After Reading

There are a number of strategies that teachers can employ at different stages of the reading process to enhance students' comprehension of the text. Those used at the pre-reading stage focus and motivate the readers and prime their brains—getting them ready for the task of reading. Strategies during the reading process actively engage their thinking and metacognition and ensure that errors in comprehension are corrected. After-reading strategies help to solidify and deepen students' understanding of the text.

Pre-Reading Instructional Strategies
Pre-reading strategies

- Help prepare the reader mentally by establishing the purpose or goal for a specific reading task.
- Activate the reader's prior knowledge about the topic and prime the brain to make connections while reading.
- Provide a quick look at the author's style, text format, level of difficulty, and major ideas.
- Hook reluctant readers and motivate them to do the hard work of reading for meaning.

Use these strategies and techniques whenever possible *before* the actual reading:

- Relate the story or informational text to the students' experience and background knowledge through class discussions, brainstorming, and charting prior knowledge ("What do we already know about . . . ?").
- Have the class make predictions prior to reading.

- Generate interest and increase students' background knowledge and frame of reference by using concrete objects and audiovisual materials related to the topic of study (maps, photos, DVDs).

- Before they read in their textbooks, give students time to survey and preview the key information: illustrations, captions, headings, and chapter questions.

- Read with students the title, headings, introduction, conclusion, and other key elements to determine topics that will be covered.

- Preview a passage by reading it aloud first. Students can then study it in a small group, with a partner, or independently.

- Introduce, pre-teach, and discuss selected vocabulary that may be challenging for students.

- Provide advance organizers—tools such as topic outlines of the content and main objectives, study guides, or graphic organizers that are provided before the student reads.

During-Reading Strategies

These strategies take place during reading. They engage students in interacting with the reading material. Engagement is crucial for comprehension, maintaining focus, and actively applying metacognition while reading.

- Teach students to paraphrase the main idea and significant details of a paragraph or section. Paraphrasing into a recorder can be very helpful for students with dyslexia.

- Indicate points throughout the text at which readers are to stop and interact with the material. At the stopping points, assign a brief task that requires readers to process what was read—for example,

- Discuss with your partner _____.
- Share with your group how you feel about _____.
- Provide each student with a pad of self-sticking notes. Have students jot down connections, notes, unfamiliar words, and questions as they read.
- Help children learn to self-monitor their comprehension while they are reading by asking themselves questions:
  - What was the main point of this section?
  - Did I understand this?
  - What part does not make sense?
  - What are the important things to remember so far?
- Model how to self-monitor comprehension and apply fix-up strategies for resolving difficulties when comprehension breaks down—for example,
  - Re-reading or scanning back through the text
  - Reading ahead to see whether one's questions are clarified later on
  - Talking with someone about points that are confusing
  - Jotting down questions to answer later
- Use cloze technique. Take a passage and delete some words, replacing them with a blank line. Students use their understanding of the text to fill in missing words. Here is an example: The boy sat on a _____ while holding the _____ tightly.
- Use advance organizers (study guides) to aid readers in looking for key information.
- Encourage children to create mental images or pictures of what is being read, given that visualization aids comprehension. Guide this process by asking questions or providing prompts such as "What do you see?" "Describe what the setting looks like."

After-Reading Strategies

After-reading strategies are used to involve readers in deeper thinking and exploration of the reading material. Here are some ideas:

- Have students use information from the text to complete charts, graphic organizers, or study guides.

- Provide sentence strips with key events of a story for students to sequence.

- Ask students to write a response to a passage of literature—an analysis of what they have read.

- Have students identify the "big idea" in what they read and the most important things to remember.

- Provide extension activities that are related to the theme and content of the reading in order to apply the learning. For example, a student may create a PowerPoint presentation after researching a topic or make a poster board that shows graphically what they have learned.

Note: Many of the strategies that are used during reading are also continued or completed after reading—for example, summaries, journal entries.

Additional Strategies to Aid Comprehension

Mnemonic Strategies

These are strategies that employ memory techniques—for example, acronyms that students learn in order to help them remember specific steps, procedures, or components.

- RAP: a paraphrasing strategy by Schumaker, Denton, & Deshler (1984):

  R: Read a paragraph.

  A: Ask yourself, "What were the main idea and details in this paragraph?"

P: Put the main idea and details in your own words.

- See the resources at end of this section for sources of learning strategies to help students with dyslexia use metacognitive skills during the reading process, and see Checklist 4.7 for more on memory strategies.

Graphic Organizers

Graphic organizers are visual aids that facilitate learning. The following types of graphic organizers are useful for increasing comprehension and recall of text.

- *Framed outlines:* Students are given copies of a teacher-prepared outline with blanks for missing information to be filled in during and after reading.

- *Storyboards:* A board or piece of paper is divided into sections, and students draw or write story events in sequence in each box or frame.

- *Story frames:* Sentence starters provide a skeleton of a story or chapter for students to fill in. Here's an example: "The setting in which this chapter takes place is _____. The character faced a problem when _____. First, he _____. Next, _____."

- *Time lines:* Students create time lines to help them visualize the chronology of a text or a sequence of events.

- *Venn diagram:* Overlapping circles are used to display differences and similarities (for example, between characters, books, settings, or events).

- *Flowchart:* A flowchart organizes a series of items or thoughts in a logical order.

- *Webs, cluster maps, and semantic maps:* A central concept or main idea is placed in the center, surrounded by related subtopics. Further details may extend from each of the subtopic areas.

Teaching the Structure of Narrative and Expository Text

- *Structure of narrative text:* Students should be taught story grammar or story mapping in order to help them understand the general structure of literary text, including setting, characters, problem or conflict, sequence of events (actions), and the resolution or problem solution.

- *Structure of expository or informational text:* Students need to be taught to identify main ideas and supportive details in the text. They also need explicit instruction on textbook features (for example, the significance of boldface and italic print, headings, and subheadings); how to use a glossary, table of contents, index, and tables and graphs; and techniques of scanning and skimming to find answers in textbooks or expository materials.

2.8 Spelling

Spelling difficulties are very common among people with dyslexia. Poor spelling affects the quality of a person's writing. By
teaching children spelling patterns and using a variety of multisensory techniques to expose them to words, students can
improve their ability to spell correctly.

Spelling and the Dyslexic Student

- Spelling (encoding) is the reverse process of decoding (reading). Decoding involves looking at letters and reading the
  sounds that they represent in order to read words. Encoding
  involves taking sounds that are heard in words and writing
  down the letter or letters that represent those sounds.

- Spelling problems in young children continue unless intervention is aimed at improving their spelling skills.

- Accurate spelling requires good phonological processing and
  phonics skills, which are areas of weakness for students with
  dyslexia.

- Because students with dyslexia often lag in development of
  phonological processing skills, they may make more spelling
  errors related to weaknesses in this area. For example, they
  may leave out letters in consonant blends (writing *boke* for
  broke or *sag* for *sang*) or put letters in the wrong sequence
  (*cats* for *cast*).

- Weak spellers may learn words for spelling tests but not
  remember the correct spelling when they are doing their
  own written work.

- Good readers are regularly exposed to written words and
  thus build an awareness of how words look in their correctly
  spelled form. Students with dyslexia often read less, so they
  have minimal visual exposure to words.

- Spelling is a more exact process than reading. To spell
  correctly, it is necessary to write the correct letters in the

correct sequence. In reading, students do not always need to read each letter because they can use context clues or recognize a word as a whole.

- A systematic, sequential approach is the most effective form of spelling instruction for students with dyslexia. Spelling work begins with one-syllable short-vowel words and continues with more complex spelling rules as students move on in school.

- To become competent spellers, students must master a sequence of skills. Students with dyslexia may take longer to master each of the spelling stages and may require more intensive instruction.

- Poor spellers may have difficulty in reading what they have written. Inaccurate spelling can have a negative impact on the way a written product is judged.

- Teaching spelling to children helps strengthen their reading skills. Learning some of the more advanced spelling concepts (such as prefixes and suffixes) aids in students' vocabulary development.

- When students are weak spellers, their written work suffers. Instead of using words they may not know how to spell, they may limit the vocabulary they use, reducing the quality and quantity of their writing.

- When students struggle with spelling, they have less mental energy to focus on what they want to say and how to organize their thoughts when writing.

- Electronic spellchecking devices are helpful tools for students with spelling difficulties. However, students should still be expected to do some written work without this type of assistance. In addition, not all spelling errors (such as using *there* instead of *their*) will be picked up by these devices, so basic spelling knowledge remains an important writing skill to develop. Handheld spellchecking devices and those on the computer do not eliminate the need for ongoing spelling instruction.

Complexities of English Spelling

At the beginning of spelling instruction, children are taught words that have a simple sound-to-letter correspondence (for example, *run*). Spelling in English becomes more complex as instruction continues, because there are many irregularities in written English. Students are asked to learn many spelling rules, as well as to spell words that are exceptions to rules that have been taught. Some of the difficulties of English spelling include the following:

- Letters can make more than one sound—for example, *g* in *gym* and *get*; *y* in *yellow*, *heavy*, and *my*.
- One sound is not always represented by a single letter; some sounds can be spelled with a combination of letters (*th*, *ph*).
- One sound can be spelled by different letters—for example, /j/ in *just*, *age*, and *fudge*.
- Vowel sounds can be represented by different spellings—for example, / ī / in *I'm*, *night*, *die*, and *fly*.
- Many English words are derived from other languages, resulting in letter combinations that may be unfamiliar to students (*mnemonic*, *chrysalis*, *physical*).

Typical Developmental Spelling Stages

Children with dyslexia go through the same developmental stages as other students, but it generally takes them much longer to do so.

1. *Pre-phonemic or preliterate—Emergent stage:* The child knows the names of some letters but does not use sound-symbol relationship or may pair a random mix of letters with pictures.
2. *Alphabetic stage:* The student knows the names of the letters, experiments with letter sounds, and may spell words with consonants only (leaving out vowels).

3. *Within-word pattern stage:* Students spell most one-syllable short-vowel words and beginning and ending consonant blends and digraphs correctly. They also use patterns and word families.

4. *Syllable and affixes stage:* Students spell most one-syllable short-vowel and long-vowel words correctly. They make errors at the syllable juncture with multisyllabic words.

5. *Derivational patterns stage:* Students are at an advanced level when most words are spelled conventionally. Misspellings involve tricky and sophisticated words.

Most third graders have reached the within-word pattern stage, and upper elementary students are generally at the syllable and affixes stage. Students with advanced phonological and word recognition ability may progress much earlier than grade-level peers. A child with dyslexia may remain in an earlier developmental stage far longer than others in his or her grade.

Methods for Teaching Spelling

- Teach the rules of spelling (for example, doubling the final consonant in a one-syllable short-vowel word before adding a suffix, as in *robbed*), providing students with logical ways to use the patterns they are learning or may already know.

- Provide more review and practice of spelling rules for students with dyslexia; they need more practice than their classmates.

- Include many manipulative activities (such as magnetic letters or letter tiles) as part of the learning process.

- Teach both regular and irregular spelling words. Although English spelling has many exceptions, good spelling instruction involves teaching students the regular patterns in addition to the irregular words that are used most frequently.

- Group words with common spelling and pronunciation features so that students have an easier time incorporating the rules they are learning.
- When modeling the process of spelling sound by sound, refer to the letters used by their sounds rather than their names.
- Teach students to break a word into syllables, then try to spell each separate syllable (*cor-re-spond*).
- Revisit newly learned words frequently, so that they are less likely to be forgotten. Point them out in reading, on the board, and in notes to students.
- Dictate sentences to students using words from current and previous spelling lists. Provide a model afterward so that students can compare their own spelling with the correct version. Dictation enables a child to make a connection between the sounds that are spoken and the written letters.
- Encourage students to discuss mistakes and figure out ways to remember the words.
- Use spelling inventories and assessment tools to determine the extent of a student's spelling knowledge as well as missing skills.
- When asking students to spell a word, have them write it down rather than try to spell it orally. In this way, students do not need to rely on memory to remember letters that they have already said. They also can look at the word to see if it looks right.
- Use weekly spelling lists to assess spelling skills. For the student with dyslexia, lists that demonstrate a common spelling pattern (for example, *light, night, fright*) are the easiest to learn.
- Construct spelling lists that match students' reading level. Students with dyslexia benefit from having individualized spelling lists that focus on their specific spelling needs.

- Teach the relationships of words (for example, *anger/angry*; *bake/baker/bakery*; *pharmacy/pharmaceutical*) so that students can use this understanding and apply it to their spelling.

- When new words are taught, provide students with opportunities to use them in their own writing as soon as possible, to reinforce their use.

- Post examples of picture associations for different phonograms for student reference. (For example, use a picture of an eagle for *ea* and a picture of a house for *ou*.)

- Post high-frequency irregular words that students are expected to spell correctly in their written work in highly visible locations. Student desk or notebook copies of such lists can be provided for reference.

- Use word walls of content-area words, high-frequency words, strategy words that illustrate spelling rules or patterns (*know*, *knife*), and other important words.

- Provide opportunities for students to work on spelling (for example, quizzing or reviewing) with a peer tutor or a partner.

Research-based programs such as those based on the Orton-Gillingham method of instruction (listed in Checklist 1.8) follow specific principles that are key to teaching students with dyslexia. Effective spelling instruction is

- *Multisensory.* Students learn by seeing, hearing, saying, and writing the words.

- *Sequential and incremental.* Instruction moves in order from simple concepts and skills to more complex ones.

- *Cumulative.* Students are engaged in ongoing review of previous concepts and words.

- *Individualized.* Instruction is customized, because students vary in their spelling acquisition skills and level of performance.

- *Explicit*. Students are taught specific spelling rules rather than being expected to figure out spelling patterns on their own.

Dictating Spelling Words

When dictating words to students:

- Model the correct pronunciation of words (perhaps exaggerating some of the sounds), especially those that students might have difficulty with (*February*, *library*), to help them correctly transcribe each sound.

- Encourage students to tap out the number of sounds they hear in the word or write a line for each sound. For example, the word *ran* would have three lines: r̲ a̲ n̲.

- Have students identify the vowel sounds in the word before writing it. They may also count out the syllables in order to guide their spelling.

- Show a correct spelling of the word after students have made their attempt to spell it.

- Model using familiar words to build new words. ("You know how to spell *rain*. Write it. Now write *train*. Now write *trainer*.")

- Have students say a word, try to spell it sound by sound orally, then try to write it.

- Encourage students to subvocalize a word, so that they say and hear each sound as they write it.

- Review the basic syllable types (see Checklist 2.3) in order to help students apply those rules in spelling.

- Introduce sight words as spelling words a few at a time, so that there are not too many to learn at once.

- Create specialized lists, if necessary, for students with spelling difficulties, focusing on specific spelling patterns or rules. Class spelling lists that are based primarily on words from a content area (for example, *pioneer, homestead, expansion*) do not have a consistent spelling pattern, so they are difficult for students with dyslexia to learn.

- Correct students' spelling once they have written the words. Teachers may encourage students to write without worrying about spelling. However, frequent corrective feedback is needed so that certain words are not misspelled out of habit or due to lack of correction.

Teaching Students How to Study Spelling Words

Bruce Murray has developed a strategy called *wordmapping* that teaches spellers to view spelling as making a map of pronunciation in order to have a more effective system for writing words correctly.

1. **Say** the word: "night"
2. **Stretch** the word: /nnn-īīī-t-t-t/
   - Work by syllables if necessary.
   - If a sound can't be stretched and held for an extended period of time like the /n/ and /ī/ sounds, then say the sound a few times—for example, /t/-/t/-/t/.
3. **Split** up the sounds.
   - Work by syllables if necessary.
   - First sound? /n/
   - Next sound? /ī/ (Repeat this step as many times as necessary.)
   - Last sound? /t/
4. **Count** the sounds: 3
5. **Draw** blanks: ⎯⎯ ⎯⎯ ⎯⎯
   - The blanks stand for the sounds.
   - Put slashes between syllables.

Next, map the spelling.

6. **Record** the spelling sound by sound.

   - On the first blank, write the letter or letters: n̲ _____ _____
   - On the next blank, write the next letters: n̲ ig̑h_____
     (Repeat this step as many times as necessary.)
   - On the last blank, write the last letters: n̲ ig̲h̲ t̲
   - If there are any silent letters in the word, place a caret
     (^) over them, as in this word nig̑ht.

7. **Study** the spelling.

   - Ask, what does [the pattern] say? In our example, what
     does *igh* say? Only ask about tricky parts.

8. **Write** the word: *night*

9. Give the **meaning.**

   - What does ——————— mean? When it's dark out.

   Source: Reprinted with permission from Bruce Murray (1999).
   Other multistep strategies for learning to spell a word
include variations such as the following:

1. Say the word.
2. Write the word while saying it.
3. Compare the word to a correct model.
4. Trace the word while saying it aloud.
5. Try to write the word from memory.
6. Check to see whether it was written correctly.

Using Multisensory Strategies to Reinforce Spelling Skills

Motivate children to practice spelling words by using engaging,
multisensory strategies in different formats:

- Writing in snow, rice, or sand placed in a shoebox top
- Finger painting words using shaving cream on tabletops or
  pudding or whipped cream on paper plates

- Writing words in glue or liquid starch on cardboard, then sprinkling the glue with glitter, beans, or macaroni to create textured, three-dimensional spelling words. (Tracing a texture with the fingers helps make a sensory imprint on a student's brain that increases memory and retention.)

- Practicing by writing words on individual chalkboards (or dry-erase boards) with colored chalk or dry-erase pens

- Writing words using alphabet manipulatives (for example, magnetic letters, sponge letters, alphabet stamps, or alphabet cereal). Students can work in large or small groups to build words. ("Let's spell the word *hot*. Now make the word *pot*. Try to spell *spot*.")

- Writing silent letters (ghost letters) in white pen

- Using the "rainbow technique" of tracing over each word at least three times in different colors with pencils, crayons, or markers, then writing the word from memory, without looking

- Using colors to highlight the tricky parts of words (*know, knee*)

- Color coding key elements of a word (for example, prefixes, suffixes, final *e*)

- Writing words by syllables in different colored markers

- Using mnemonics whenever possible to help remember and learn memory strategies. For example, to spell *friend*, remember "I am a friEND to the END; to spell *principal*, remember "The princiPAL is your PAL."

- Playing games that involve spelling: Hangman, Scrabble, Boggle (Parker Brothers)

- Creating pictures using words. (For example, write *look* with the *o*'s drawn as eyes; write *clown* and then draw a funny hat on top.)

Using Song and Movement to Practice Spelling Words

- Pair a movement with spelling words aloud (clap to each letter, bounce a ball, use a yo-yo, jump rope).

- Tap out the sounds or syllables in a word (pencil to desk, fingertips to arm).
- Have students spell words while standing up for consonant letters and sitting down for vowels.

Other Ways to Help Students Practice, Study, and Learn the Spelling of Words

- Have students make flash cards, then study each of the words with a partner (or parent), putting aside the words that were missed so that they can be studied again later.
- Make up word skeletons—for example, ____ ____ s ____ r ____ ____ e ____ t for the word *instrument*. Have students fill in the missing letters.
- Teach the "Look, Say, Write" method of practice: "Look at the word and trace it with your finger or your pencil. Say the word. Spell it out loud while you copy it. Now, write the word without looking. Check it against the one you traced. Did you write it correctly? If you made a mistake, fix it now, and think of a way to remember the correct spelling."
- Use word sorts to provide opportunities for students to discover common patterns. For example, students would place *stopping, sitting,* and *cutting* in one column, while *reading, playing,* and *sorting* would go in another column. Have students state the spelling rules for each column.
- See Checklist 2.16, "The Basic Spelling Vocabulary List," created by Steven Graham, Karen Harris, and Connie Loynachan. This list was constructed for teachers to use in selecting spelling words for students to learn during the year. The list, subdivided into lists for grades 1–5, contains the 850 words that children use most often in their own writing. The words with asterisks are considered more difficult words for children to spell. Learning to spell these words correctly will help improve the quality of a child's writing.

2.9 Common Writing Difficulties for Children with Dyslexia

Many students with dyslexia are capable of orally sharing a wealth of information on a topic or articulating a creative, detailed story but cannot effectively communicate their ideas in writing. Using written language can be very challenging and frustrating. It is a complex process involving numerous skills and brain processes, some of which are areas of weakness for those with dyslexia.

The writing process requires

- *Awareness:* When students are given a writing assignment such as an essay, they must draw upon awareness of
  - Background knowledge on the topic
  - How to research relevant information on the topic
  - The specific structure for the genre assigned (persuasive essay, narrative account, response to literature)
  - What the teacher wants in the paper—the performance standards and expectations to be met

  Students with dyslexia often lack awareness in these areas. Because they generally read fewer high-quality texts than their classmates, they have often had less exposure to good models of written language.

- *Skills and brain processes:* Producing a writing assignment requires a student to use multiple skills, many of which are areas of weakness for dyslexic learners, including organization, language, memory and sequencing, metacognition, processing speed, perceptual-motor skills, and attention. (See more information on these types of weaknesses in Checklists 1.3 and 1.5.)

Steps of the Writing Process and Potential Problems

When asked to write a paragraph, report, or essay, students are taught to follow these steps:

- *Prewrite:* Before beginning the actual writing, students need to brainstorm and gather ideas, select a topic, and organize information according to the required form, often on a visual organizer or other planning sheet. Children with dyslexia may get stuck at this stage; they may find it difficult to know what to write about or how to gather information, narrow a topic, or organize and sequence ideas. (See Checklist 2.10 for prewriting strategies and supports.)

- *Draft:* Writing a draft involves turning ideas from the planning stage into written sentences, adding details, and elaborating. At this stage, spelling, mechanics, or neatness are not important, as long as the writer can read his or her own work. However, for students with dyslexia, poor spelling can be immobilizing. In addition, they often have difficulty expressing ideas in complete sentences that flow and make effective transitions while conveying what they want to say.

  - Lack of fluency in spelling and mechanics
  - Weaknesses in memory, language, and metacognitive awareness
  - Slow processing or production speed can impair a dyslexic writer's efficiency in turning prewriting plans into a viable first draft. (See Checklist 2.11 for drafting and composition strategies and supports.)

- *Revise:* Once an initial draft is completed, students need to understand that a number of changes will be needed before a writing project is in its final form. When writing is a struggle and a first draft has been produced, students may resist making revis\ions, such as additions, deletions, or movement of words, sentences, or paragraphs. Revising requires the ability to self-monitor one's work and to re-read it and identify ways to improve flow and sequence, language usage, and clarity— difficult tasks for students with dyslexia. (See Checklist 2.12 for strategies and supports to use during the revision process.)

- *Edit:* Editing is the proofreading stage of writing. Identifying grammatical, spelling, and mechanical (capitalization and punctuation) errors, and then fixing them, is a tedious task for someone with dyslexia. It is unrealistic to expect students with dyslexia to edit their work without direct assistance (such as adult or peer editing or the use of assistive technology). (See Checklist 2.12 for editing strategies and supports.)

- *Publish:* The last stage of the writing process is completing and sharing the final product. When a student feels proud of a piece of writing and shares it, this part of the process is rewarding.

While students with dyslexia can benefit greatly from numerous strategies that can be implemented throughout the writing process, they may also benefit from accommodations and interventions to alleviate or bypass some problems they experience while writing. (See Checklists 2.13 and 2.14 for written language accommodations and information on assistive technology.)

2.10 Strategies to Help with Prewriting: Planning and Organizing

Prewriting is a critical stage of the writing process that involves generation, planning, and organization of ideas. These tasks are a challenge for many students with dyslexia. It is important to provide instruction and support to guide students in the kind of thinking and questioning that is needed to effectively plan for writing.

Prewriting Techniques for the Classroom

- *Brainstorming:* Sessions are short and focused. Given a general theme or topic, students call out whatever comes to mind while someone records responses. Follow whole-group brainstorming with partner or small-group sharing.

- *Quick writes:* Students have three or four minutes to write down everything that they can think of about a topic. Following this activity, students can share what they wrote with a partner or a group.

- *Keeping a folder of writing topics:* Students maintain a folder, card file, or notebook of ideas for writing topics. These might include hobbies, places visited, jobs they have done, or colorful and interesting people they know. A writing folder can also be a personal collage. Students can use words and pictures cut from magazines, newspapers, and travel brochures and laminate the folder.

- *Keeping a computer file of writing topics*: Students use a computer file to record their writing ideas. The file might include digital pictures of people, objects, interesting items, or topics found on Web sites.

- *Telling personal stories:* In small groups, students tell personal stories in response to prompts—for example, "Tell about a time you or someone you knew got lost." After sharing stories in small groups, students fill out graphic organizers, then write rough drafts or outlines of their stories.

- *Writing prompts:* A stimulus is provided, such as a story, picture, or song, to prompt writing.

- *Story starters and sample topic sentences:* For students who continue to struggle to find ideas, providing a choice of topic sentences or a story starter (a sentence or two to introduce a topic) might be helpful.

- *Looking at reference books:* Students can browse many kinds of books in order to gather ideas for writing topics (for example, mysteries of nature, music, sports, fashion).

- *Verbalizing ideas into a recording device:* Some students benefit from talking into a digital recorder and then transcribing their ideas.

- *Sharing exemplary and at-standard pieces of writing:* To help students generate ideas of their own as well as understand the structure of a particular genre, read them some good examples. Read aloud (and project with an overhead projector or document camera) some pieces of student writing and then discuss them.

- *Modeled writing:* Model the process of brainstorming, organizing, and recording ideas.

- *Frames:* Providing frames helps struggling writers get started and guides them in planning. Example: "I remember my first day of _____ when I was _____ years old. I felt _____ ."

Using Visual Organization Strategies Prior to Writing

Graphic organizers are effective in helping writers formulate their ideas as well as organize thoughts and information. Following are some examples of graphic organizers. Others can be found in Checklist 2.7.

- *Clustering:* Write the main idea in a box in the center of the page and surround the main idea box with bubbles containing supporting ideas.

- *Mind mapping, or webbing:* A circle is drawn around a topic in the center of a page. Related ideas are written on lines radiating from the circle.

- *Software organizers:* Software can facilitate the creation of mind maps, diagrams, and other visual organizers to aid in prewriting. Two such programs are Inspiration™ and Kidspiration™ from www.inspiration.com.

- *Cards or strips:* Have students write main ideas and supporting details on separate index cards or sentence strips. This method makes it easier to spread out, organize, and sequence ideas.

Some Web sites that have free downloadable graphic organizers include Masterminds Publishing's site at www .graphicorganizers.com and Houghton Mifflin's Education Place at www.eduplace.com.

Graphic organizers should follow the format for the type of writing required: narrative (tells a story); expository (explains, reports, or informs); persuasive (tries to persuade or convince); or descriptive (describes something).

Thinking and Questioning

- Provide a prewriting checklist with specific questions for students to ask themselves at this stage of the writing process. These questions will help the writer think through, plan, and organize ideas prior to drafting. Questioning can be done independently or with someone else (a peer partner, a parent, or a teacher).

- When creating a prewriting checklist, use questions like these:

  - Who is my target audience?

  - What is my purpose? To persuade? Inform? Entertain?

  - What do I already know about this topic?

  - What are some words or ideas related to my topic?

How Parents Can Help Children Think of Writing Topics

- Look through family albums together. Discuss people and events.

- Talk about events in your child's life (humorous incidents, scary moments, milestones).

- Share family stories and discuss current events.

- Ask leading questions that encourage your child to share his or her feelings, fears, and dreams.

- Provide resources such as books, reference materials, access to a library, and access to the Internet.

- Encourage your child to maintain a journal or a computer file in which to jot down thoughts or questions, observations, reactions to events in the news or events in his or her life, or connections between movies or books and his or her own life. Any of these are possible topics for future writing assignments.

2.11 Strategies for Teaching Composition and Written Expression

Written expression is a common academic area of difficulty among students with dyslexia. Many skills are used simultaneously when trying to compose a written piece: language, memory, sequencing, organization, planning, self-monitoring, critical thinking, and language mechanics (capitalization, punctuation, spelling). Some of these skills are particularly weak in children with dyslexia. Students are expected to meet grade-level standards in several writing formats and genres, such as persuasive essays, personal narratives, summaries, and reports. Teachers have the challenge of differentiating instruction to writers of varying levels.

Even students with significant writing difficulties are able to meet writing standards when they receive explicit teaching and modeling of writing skills and strategies. They benefit from guided assistance as they proceed through the writing process. Struggling writers need more intensive, explicit instruction and practice than their peers to develop their skills as writers.

The craft of writing and composing can be taught using some of these approaches:

- *Modeled writing:* Demonstrate the use of strategies, allowing students to witness the thinking and self-questioning processes that are used while composing. Speak aloud what you are thinking (metacognition) while creating a draft of some piece of writing—for example, a beginning paragraph with an interesting lead. Project your writing on a screen so that students can follow the process.

- *Student examples:* Have student volunteers share parts of what they are writing to provide examples for the class. Student sharing in front of the whole class should be done only by volunteers (unless the work is in its final form).

- *Guided writing:* Work with students in groups that are differentiated in various ways, such as skill level or degree of assistance needed, topic chosen, or stage of the writing process. Some students in the class may be writing a single cohesive paragraph while others are composing multiple paragraphs. As students are drafting, circulate among the groups, observing, asking questions, listening to students as they share, and offering guidance and instruction as needed.

- *Sensory descriptions:* Teach students through modeling and by sharing descriptive examples from literature, helping the reader to feel, hear, see, taste, and smell through words.

- *Sentence starters:* Provide a list of sentence starters that students can use to help them remember to include important points, such as evidence and support for their statements, in their writing. For example, "This was demonstrated when _____.")

- *Topic sentences:* Help students who have difficulty getting started by providing a list of possible sentence starters or topic sentences.

- *Frames:* Provide writing frames for scaffolding or support. Example: "The author, _____ (*insert name*) wrote a/an _____ (*insert genre*) titled _____ (*title*), which took place _____ (*where and when*)."

- *Explaining genres:* Model and explain the structure and format for each genre taught.

- *Rubrics:* Provide rubrics (scoring guides) with all writing assignments. Rubrics explain the performance standards for the assignment and what is expected for elements such as content, organization, mechanics, or neatness in order to meet or exceed grade-level standards. Rubrics are particularly helpful for students with writing difficulties and their parents, teachers, and tutors because they explain exactly what is expected in the assignment and describe the criteria for proficiency.

- Rubrics typically use a scale of 1 to 4 or 1 to 5 (for example, 1 = Novice, 2 = Apprentice, 3 = Practitioner, 4 = Expert).

- Teachers can create their own rubric that is specific to an assignment or use generic ones for a specific genre. Rubrics can also be found on the Internet—for example, at www.rubistar.4teachers.org.

- *Monitoring:* Provide support for children with dyslexia, who often take much longer to complete writing assignments than other students. Getting them started early, notifying parents of the requirements, and jointly monitoring throughout the assignment are very helpful.

- *Instructional programs:* Take advantage of the many programs that help teachers explicitly instruct students on how to write in various genres and build written composition skills through a structured approach with multisensory tools. Such programs scaffold learning through step-by-step approaches, graphic organizers, color coding, and other means, in order to enhance the craft of writing. For example, see the writing programs by Auman (2008), Mariconda and Auray (2005), and Fetzer (2003). See also the resources listed at end of this section for more information on programs.

- *Customizing your own approach:* Experiment with a variety of strategies and instructional tools. Web sites in the online resources listed at the end of this section have additional writing strategies and suggestions.

Teaching Sentence Structure and Expanded Word Choices

- Teach sentence structure and build sentence-writing skills. Children need to understand that all complete sentences have (1) a *subject* (a noun: a person, place, or thing) that tells who or what is doing something, and (2) a *predicate* (a verb or prepositional phrases) that tell about the subject.

- Teach children to write interesting, expanded sentences. Start with a simple sentence (for example, *The puppy cried.*). Have them dress it up by adding or substituting descriptive adjectives and adverbs, more powerful verbs, and prepositional phrases (When? Where? How? Why?). Example: *The frightened puppy whimpered and whined as it hid, shaking, under the sofa during the thunderstorm.*

- Teach students to use descriptive language that will enhance their writing style. Generate class and individual lists of descriptive and figurative language found in literature or poetry—for example,

  - Metaphors (comparisons such as these examples: *The room is an oven. His temper is an unpredictable thunderstorm.*)

  - Similes (comparisons using the word *like* or *as*, such as *helpless as a newborn baby*)

  - Onomatopoeia (words that echo sounds, such as *sizzle, crack, pop*).

- Post lists and provide desk or notebook copies for reference of transition or linking words and phrases. For example:

  - Words that signal sequence: *first of all, furthermore, later*

  - Words that signal comparison and contrast of two or more things: *nevertheless, conversely*

  - Words that signal cause and effect: *consequently, as a result*

  - Words that indicate an author's point of view: *I suggest, I believe*

- See Checklist 2.6 for strategies to teach figurative language, precision in word choice, and other means of enhancing expressive writing.

Teaching Students to Compose a Draft

- Help students with writing by teaching them to prepare effectively. When students write their initial draft, a graphic organizer or planning sheet filled out at the prewriting stage should be their guide. They should already know their audience, genre structure, topic, point of view, sequence (for a narrative piece) or main idea and supporting details (for an informational piece).

- Have students write their rough drafts in pencil or erasable pen.

- For students who prefer a computer and those entitled to assistive technology for writing, be sure one is provided.

- If students are typing drafts, show them how to save each successive draft with a new date or draft number and how to back up their work. Handwritten drafts should be dated.

- Provide a scribe for students who have trouble getting their thoughts written down.

- If students are having difficulty with writing, suggest that they start in the middle. Students with dyslexia may get stuck on the introductory paragraph and may do better if, after the initial planning, they write some of the other paragraphs first. They can work on an introductory paragraph and conclusion later.

- When assigning an essay, particularly in response to questions or a prompt, ensure that students understand what is being asked and what needs to be addressed in their essay. First, carefully read and analyze the prompt or question. If students have difficulty doing so, provide help.

Teaching Self-Monitoring

Written expression requires considerable self-monitoring. Writers should put themselves in the place of their potential readers and keep asking themselves questions such as "Does this make sense?" "Is this clear?" "Do my ideas flow logically?" "Am I using the best choice of words?"

- Provide students with a checklist of self-monitoring questions to use as a guide in writing different types of compositions.
- Teach students to use learning strategies such as OSWALD and WRITE, which provide steps to follow in composing an essay:
  - OSWALD (from James Madison University Special Education Program's Learning Toolbox at http://coe.jmu.edu/learningtoolbox):

    Outline the major points and details that you want to include in your paper.

    Say the outline aloud. Read the outline over to see the relationship between ideas. As you read the outline, think of the main ideas that are most important to your paper.

    Write an introduction, a paragraph introducing your paper. Include the main ideas that you chose when you read the outline aloud.

    Add connecting ideas. Write sentences to connect ideas from one paragraph to another. Think of words that help show the relationship between ideas (for example, *therefore*, *after*).

    Look over the connections. Re-read your paper, starting with the introduction. Make sure that each paragraph is connected to the introduction and to the other paragraphs.

    Draft conclusion. Based on your introduction and the ideas presented in the body of your paper, write an ending that wraps up the ideas.
  - WRITE (Harris, Graham, Mason, Friedlander, & Reid, 2007) is a helpful acronym for the steps of writing:

    Work from your plan to develop your thesis statement. Start with an attention getter.

Remember your goals (mature vocabulary, organization, varied sentence types, maintaining topic control).

Include a transition word for each paragraph.

Try to use different kinds of sentences.

Exciting, interesting words

See the resources at the end of this section for sources of other learning strategies.

2.12 Strategies to Help with Revising and Editing

Revising written work involves adding or deleting information, re-sequencing the order of sentences and paragraphs, and choosing words that better communicate your meaning. Revision requires self-monitoring and critically evaluating one's own work. These skills are often difficult for students with dyslexia to master. Understandably, they are resistant to making changes once a first draft is written.

Students need to understand that a draft is only a first attempt at writing and that the process of writing often involves several revisions before it is complete. Students with dyslexia need direct instruction, modeling, and feedback in order to learn how to revise their work.

Editing involves proofreading for errors in grammar, mechanics, and spelling and then polishing the final product. Students with dyslexia are typically very weak in editing skills. It is unrealistic to expect they will be able to adequately proofread for their own errors and fix them without direct help, such as teacher, parent, or peer editing or assistive technology supports.

Strategies for Helping Students with Revision

- Encourage students to write rough drafts on every other line of the paper in double-space format, to make it easier to revise and edit.
- Allow students to compose on a computer in double-space format, which is ideal for revising subsequent drafts. Another benefit of composing on a computer is being able to save various draft versions electronically rather than storing them on paper. Electronic storage can be a significant help in students' organization and management of written work.
- Model and demonstrate the steps for revising—one step at a time.
- Provide checklists to help students self-monitor during the revision process. Select *some* (not all) of the following

questions in creating a list appropriate to the developmental level of the child.

- Does my introduction capture the attention of my readers?
- Did I develop my ideas logically?
- Have I given enough information?
- Does everything make sense?
- Did I stick to my topic?
- Have I presented my ideas clearly and in the right order?
- Have I given details and examples for each main idea?
- Do I need to insert, move around, or delete any ideas?
- Have I used interesting descriptive words?
- Do my paragraphs have a beginning, middle, and end?
- Have I replaced overused words?
- Did I write an interesting, powerful conclusion?

- Have students read their drafts to a peer in order to obtain feedback. The partner listens, asks questions, indicates when more information is needed, and makes other suggestions. Parents can also provide feedback in order to help their child learn to make appropriate revisions. Information can be inserted with carets ^ or on sticky notes next to where it will be added.

- When a student is revising a composition, suggest that he or she address one aspect of the writing at a time. For example, a student could focus first on clarity (which includes flow and sequence), then read for sentence variety and descriptive language, and next for overused words.

- Teach the skill of combining sentences, and encourage this technique when students are revising. Example: *The day was hot and sunny. The girls ate ice cream cones. They played and rode their bikes.* These three sentences can be combined: *The girls ate ice cream cones, played, and rode their bikes on the hot, sunny day.*

- During the revision process, have students identify sentences that can be improved. Encourage them to find boring, simple sentences and embellish them.

- When listening to a child read an initial draft, provide positive feedback by describing something you like about the piece, acknowledging the student's growth in a specific skill, or recognizing the student's effort. Ask probing questions when something is unclear and more information is needed.

- If revising is overwhelming for the student, consider providing a scribe. Let children dictate the changes they want to make, and have the scribe record those changes on the paper.

Strategies for Helping Students with Editing

- Provide direct instruction and guided practice in the proper use of mechanics (for example, punctuation and capitalization).

- Have students use peer editing as well as adult assistance. A peer or adult partner can point out run-on or incomplete sentences, missing or incorrect capitalization or punctuation, and misspelled words.

- Teach students how to use editing tools and options (thesaurus, spellcheck, cut and paste) on a word processor.

- Even though self-editing is hard, encourage it by having students circle (or code) words that they think are misspelled. Later, with assistance as needed, they can go back and check the spelling.

- Provide the use of an electronic spellchecking device for home and school. Handheld devices are available as well as spellchecking tools on word processors. (See Checklist 2.13.)

- Teach editing symbols (insert, delete, capitalize, new paragraph). Provide reference charts that show those symbols.

- After modeling how to jointly edit a piece of writing for the whole class, have students work in pairs to check each other's work.

- Have students use colored pencils as they edit for one thing at a time. For example, have them check each sentence and underline the final punctuation in red, capital letters in blue.
- Provide an editing checklist to help students proofread their own work for capitalization, sentence structure, and mechanical errors. Following is a list of possible questions to include in a proofreading checklist:
  - Did I use complete sentences?
  - Did I begin all sentences with capital letters?
  - Did I end sentences with a final punctuation mark (., ?, !)?
  - Have I capitalized all proper nouns?
  - Have I checked spelling?
  - Have I indented my paragraphs?
  - Are verb tenses consistent?
  - Are there run-on sentences?
  - Is my paper neat and organized?

Other Tips for Helping Students with Their Writing

- Conduct teacher-student writing conferences in which students respond to their own writing. ("My best sentence is _____." "A simile or metaphor I used was _____.") The student reflects on his or her own work. Student and teacher share what they like about the writing.
- Have students evaluate where they have improved and skills to target for continued improvement. ("My writing has improved in _____ [sentence structure, paragraphing, organization, punctuation, spelling]. I plan to work on _____.")
- Provide a rubric with all writing assignments. Show models of work that are standard and that exceed the standard.

- Teach students who are drafting on a computer how to find overused words that they might want to replace. With the control-F function, they can type in the word and quickly find it throughout the document, so that it can be replaced.

- Use the track changes and comment features in Microsoft Word. Another reader (parent, teacher, peer) can make comments and note suggested changes in the file of a draft that a student has written on a computer.

Learning Strategies

Strategies that incorporate mnemonic techniques to remember steps of a strategy and apply them independently are powerful for students with dyslexia. Here are two learning strategies for revision and editing:

- *COPS* is an error-monitoring strategy (Schumaker, Nolan, & Deshler, 1985). A writer reads through his or her work four times, each time checking the writing for one of the four components in the following list and correcting errors.

  Capitalize: Have I capitalized the first word of each sentence and all proper nouns?

  Overall: How is the overall appearance (spacing, indentation, neatness)?

  Punctuation: Have I put in commas, semicolons, and end punctuation?

  Spelling: Have I spelled the words correctly?

- *SCOPE* is a learning strategy for proofreading from Learning Toolbox at James Madison University Special Education Program Web site (http://coe.jmu.edu/learningtoolbox). The student reads the paper five times, each time looking for a different type of error.

  Spelling. Re-read your paper for misspelled words.

    Use a spelling checker. Try writing misspelled words

in different ways to see if one looks right. Use a dictionary to find correct spellings.

Capitalization. Re-read your paper to make sure all words
are correctly capitalized.

Order of words. Read your paper aloud. Point to each word
as you say it to make sure that no words have been omit-
ted, added, or mixed up.

Punctuation. Re-read your paper to check for correct
punctuation.

Express complete thoughts. Re-read each sentence aloud
to make sure that sentences are grammatically correct.
(Each sentence should have a complete thought; there
should be no run-on sentences; and all parts of the sentence should agree.) The sentences should sound right.

See Checklist 2.11 and the resources at the end of this section for more learning strategies for students to use in their
writing.

2.13 Assistive Technology to Support Reading and Writing

Many reading and writing difficulties that students with dyslexia experience can be alleviated significantly with assistive technology that is now available. Many technological tools and resources for home and school are affordable and accessible.

An assistive technology device is any item, piece of equipment, or product system used to increase, maintain, or improve the functional capabilities of individuals with a disability. Students with dyslexia who qualify for assistive technology under IDEA or Section 504 have that fact documented in their Individualized Education Plan (IEP) or 504 accommodation plan. (See Checklists 5.4, 5.5, and 5.6, which explain and discuss IEPs and Section 504 plans for eligible students with disabilities.) Assistive technology equipment or services designated in their plan are provided by the school district.

Audio Books

- Audio books (which used to be referred to as *books on tape*)—recordings of books or other text—are an excellent support for people with dyslexia, as they are enabled to access text that they cannot read on their own.
- Numerous books are in audio format, and many are available through public library systems.
- Audio textbooks in all content areas and grade levels are available to students who qualify as having a reading disability severe enough to prevent them from accessing printed material in the standard manner.

Electronic Text (E-Text or E-Books)

Electronic text (books or other text presented in digital format)

- Is highly beneficial for students with dyslexia because it can be altered in various ways (enlarged, changed in color or font, converted to other formats, copied and transferred to other documents, read with talking software)
- Is highly interactive and engaging
- Often uses multimedia enhancements such as graphics, animations, rollover features or other easy access to definitions of words or explanations of concepts, or links to related information

Audio Books and E-Text Services for Students with Dyslexia

- Many students with dyslexia are eligible for textbooks and other books and written material in e-text or audio book format. Recording for the Blind and Dyslexic (RFB&D) and Bookshare.org are two organizations that provide such materials to students with disabilities who meet qualification requirements.
  - **Recording for the Blind and Dyslexic** (www.rfbd.org), a nonprofit organization, is the nation's educational library, serving people who cannot read standard print effectively because of a visual impairment, learning disability, or other disability. It lends audio books (including student textbooks) in a broad range of subjects at all levels, from kindergarten to postgraduate studies. To access their library, one must be eligible and become a member. Textbooks are available on CD through RFB&D's AudioPlus® service. In order to play digitally recorded textbooks, students need a specialized CD player or software available for purchase through RFB&D. For information, contact your district's special education department or visit the RFB&D Web site at www.rfbd.org.

- **Bookshare.org** (www.bookshare.org) is an online community that enables people with visual and other print disabilities to legally share scanned books. Bookshare .org produces electronic text in the form of downloadable digital talking book versions of printed materials. A text-to-speech player is provided to members. Membership is free for all U.S. students with qualifying disabilities. Individual memberships can also be purchased. Membership provides disabled readers unlimited access to the world's largest online library of accessible reading materials (books, textbooks, newspapers, and magazines).

- Check with members of a student's IEP team or with local or regional assistive technology specialists regarding eligibility requirements for any of the organizations mentioned in this list.

- For information and advice on obtaining audio books or e-text materials, refer to these articles from the Center for Applied Special Technology and LD Online:

  - "Reading Rockets: An Educator's Guide to Making Textbooks Accessible and Usable for Students with Learning Disabilities"

    http://www.readingrockets.org/article/16310

  - "Accessible Textbooks: A Guide for Parents of Children with Learning Disabilities"

    http://www.readingrockets.org/article/16308

Word Processing

The use of computers and word processing has revolutionized the way we write. To be freed from the task of handwriting and to be able to easily save drafts of work, revise by cutting and pasting, edit with tools such as spellcheck and grammar check, and produce easy-to-read copies are satisfying to both writer and reader. Knowing that it is relatively easy to revise, reorganize, replace vocabulary, and correct spelling and grammar enables writers to focus on the content and produce better writing. Learning how to use word processing with proficiency needs to be a priority for students with dyslexia.

Portable Word Processors

- NEO (www.neo-direct.com) is a popular portable word processor and assistive technology tool. It is the newer version that has replaced the AlphaSmart (now owned by the company Renaissance Learning Inc.), which had been used successfully by students with writing disabilities for a number of years. These word processors are popular because of their low cost, simplicity, and extreme durability. They have a very long battery life, full-sized keyboard, and weigh under two pounds. NEO comes with a variety of functions (dictionary, thesaurus, spellchecker), and optional add-ons are available, such as text-to-speech and advanced word prediction. Other benefits are the ability to turn them on and off instantly and easily transfer written work from the word processor to a Mac or PC via a USB cable.

- Dana http://www.neo-direct.com/Dana/ is a palm-powered writing tool. It is part word processor and part PDA (handheld computer). One can write a story, organize the week, record an appointment, or read an eBook from anywhere. Dana offers up to twenty-five hours of runtime on a single charge and is fully compatible with Microsoft Word, Excel, and PowerPoint file formats.

Typing and Keyboarding Software and Programs

To get the most out of word processing, a person must learn keyboarding skills. It is recommended that training and practice in keyboarding be provided to students with dyslexia. Children vary in their readiness to learn keyboarding skills. Many benefit from keyboarding training in third or fourth grade. Some software programs for learning keyboarding are listed here, along with the companies that sell them.

- Type to Learn (Sunburst)
- Mario Teaches Typing 2 (Brainstorm)
- JumpStart Typing (Knowledge Adventure)
- Mavis Beacon Teaches Typing (The Learning Company)
- Look and Learn Keyboard Typing System (KeyWrite)
- UltraKey (Bytes of Learning, Inc.)
- Typing Instructor Deluxe (Individual Software)
- Typing Time (Thomson Learning/South-Western Educational Publishing)
- Keyboarding for Individual Achievement (Teachers' Institute for Special Education).

Online typing programs such as Dance Mat Typing (www .bbc.co.uk/schools/typing) are also available.

Word Predictors and Spelling Checkers

- Word predictors analyze words as they are written on the computer, then try to predict the words that the user is most likely to want from a dictionary or lexicon of words. As the writer types a letter of the alphabet, the program offers a list of the most common words beginning with that letter. If the first letter does not bring up the right word, more choices are offered when a second letter is typed. Some programs speak the words from the list out loud to help the writer select the desired word.
- Spelling checkers are very helpful for writers with spelling difficulties. Many software programs that are designed for struggling readers and writers have word prediction and spellchecking functions with an audio component

(Co-Writer, Write:OutLoud®, Read & Write Gold, WordQ™, and SpeakQ™). The word choices are read aloud from the computer to make it easier for the user to identify the appropriate word.

- Ghotit Context Spellchecker Service (www.ghotit.com) is a set of services designed specifically for dyslexic adults and children whose spelling and typing errors are too far from the correct spelling of the word or out of context to benefit from regular spelling checkers.

Text-to-Speech Software

- A number of programs can read text (from books, text documents, or the Internet) aloud from the computer. Text-to-speech software enables students to see the print (digitized text) highlighted as they hear it being read aloud. Some examples of text-to-speech software include Read & Write Gold, ClaroRead Plus, Kurzweil 3000, Read: OutLoud®, and ReadPlease®.

- Some software for writing such as Write:OutLoud® and Read & Write Gold TextHelp programs have text-to-speech features, which are helpful to students with dyslexia, particularly during the revision and editing stages of writing.

Speech Recognition Systems

- Speech recognition systems enable users to control a computer by speaking to it, allowing them to enter text or issue commands (for example, to load a particular program or to print a document). Speech recognition supports individuals with writing disabilities; they can dictate thoughts when composing and have oral language automatically converted into print.

- Speech recognition systems require training the computer to recognize the user's voice.
- Dragon Naturally Speaking and SpeakQ™ are examples of two programs with speech recognition systems.

Sources for Assistive Technology

Following is a list of companies that specialize in assistive software and other technology to enhance skills and support challenged readers and writers. Some of their products are also listed.

- Don Johnston: SOLO software programs Co-Writer, DraftBuilder, Write:OutLoud, and Read:OutLoud (a text reader)
  www.donjohnston.com
- EnableMart: ClaroRead Plus, Quicktionary Reading Pen
  www.enablemart.com
- Franklin Electronic Publishers: handheld electronic dictionaries, spelling checkers, and other reference devices
  www.franklin.com
- Freedom Scientific: WYNN Reader
  www.freedomscientific.com
- Inspiration: Inspiration and Kidspiration (software)
  www.inspiration.com
- Kurzweil Educational Systems: Kurzweil 3000
  www.kurzweiledu.com
- Nuance: Dragon Naturally Speaking
  www.nuance.com
- Quillsoft Ltd.: WordQ™ and SpeakQ™
  www.quillsoft.com and www.wordq.com
- ReadPlease: ReadPlease®
  www.readplease.com

- TextHelp: Read & Write GOLD
  www.texthelp.com
- Wiz Com Technologies: Reading Pen
  www.wizcomtech.com

Web Sites on Assistive Technology

Some sites that provide information on assistive technology to support individuals with disabilities include these:

- Alliance for Technology Access
  www.ataccess.org
- Family Center on Technology and Disability
  www.fctd.info/resources
- Families and Advocates Partnership for Education
  www.fape.org
- Great Schools (formerly Schwab Learning)
  www.greatschools.net
- LD Online
  www.ldonline.org
- Reading Rockets
  www.readingrockets.org

See the resources at end of this section for reading intervention software and online programs.

2.14 Accommodating Reading and Writing Difficulties

Teachers need to be flexible and willing to make accommodations and provide the necessary supports for students with dyslexia to help them achieve success. If a student has an IEP or Section 504 plan, teachers are required under federal law to provide the accommodations that are written in their plan.

Accommodations to Help Students in Reading

- Present text orally. Read it aloud or assign a classmate or peer tutor to read the material with a struggling reader, enabling him or her to access grade-level and advanced material.

- Color code a master textbook copy that students can borrow. This book will be used to indicate the most important information for students to learn. (For example, key vocabulary terms might be highlighted in pink, facts and main ideas in yellow.)

- Provide reading material and resources at an appropriate level for independent reading through a leveled library or a selection of high-interest books with easy vocabulary.

- Code leveled books discretely so that it is not obvious to classmates when a student has selected an "easy" book for independent reading.

- Provide books on the same theme or topic (such as the solar system or biographies of presidents) as the books that other students are reading, but at a lower reading level.

- Allow students who need auditory input or have trouble maintaining attention when reading silently to go to a quiet corner to read aloud to themselves or into a whisper-phone (a curved, hollow plastic tube held like a telephone). When reading into a whisper-phone, a child clearly hears his or her own voice without disturbing others. One such device is the Toobaloo (available at www.superduperinc.com). Whisper-phones can also be constructed with two elbow-shaped PVC pipes.

- Provide assistive technology such as recorded books or text-to-speech software to enable students with reading disabilities to access grade-level and advanced material. (See Checklist 2.13.)

- Provide advance organizers such as study guides or outlines of main ideas to support comprehension of reading material.

- Preview and discuss difficult vocabulary that will be encountered in the reading.

- Provide audio recordings of literature and textbook chapters that are to be read in class.

- Reduce the amount of reading required in assignments that use grade-level material.

- Provide a photocopy of important pages so that students can write in the margins, underline, or highlight important information with colored markers.

- Allow the use of a cardboard strip, window frame, or other markers that help students keep their place while reading.

- Record readings from textbook pages and allow students to listen to them.

- Provide an extra set of books for a student to keep at home.

- Do not require a student with dyslexia to read aloud in front of others.

- Read directions aloud to students and follow up by checking to make sure that students understand what they are being asked to do.

- Provide cue cards or lists of fix-up strategies that students can try when they do not understand something.

- See Checklists 2.2 through 2.7 for more reading accommodations and supports.

Accommodations to Help Students in Writing

- Reduce the need to copy from the board or book. Provide photocopies of notes or material instead.

- Make adjustments in order to accept modified homework that requires reduced amounts of writing. Discuss the adjustments ahead of time with students and parents.

- Substitute nonwritten, hands-on assignments and oral presentations for written assignments.

- Enlarge the space for doing written work on math papers, tests, and worksheets.

- Stress the accuracy and quality of writing, not the volume.

- Permit students to dictate responses and have someone else (an adult, classmate, or cross-age tutor) be a scribe and write down what the student says.

- Allow students to print or use cursive handwriting.

- Provide note-taking assistance. Assign students who need assistance a buddy to take notes and share and compare information.

- Provide partial outlines or frames in which the student fills in the missing information while listening to lectures.

- Provide NCR (non-carbon replica) paper so that copies of notes can be easily shared with students with learning disabilities who have trouble taking notes. The student who takes the notes receives the top copy. The bottom copy can be torn off and given to a student with dyslexia. Alternatively, notes can be photocopied. Encourage students to take their own notes, but allow them to supplement their own notes with more detailed, organized copies from the note taker.

- Teach keyboarding and word processing skills, or suggest that students learn by using a software program at home.

- Provide students with assistance with typing and printing final drafts of papers.

- When writing in class is required, allow students with learning disabilities to take extra time as needed, particularly on essay questions for written assessments.

- On writing assignments, grade content and mechanics separately.

- Provide graphic organizers or other structural aids for written assignments.

- Allow students to use a digital recorder instead of writing in order to summarize learning, respond to questions, plan, or record ideas and instructions.

- If a child struggles to hold a pencil, have him or her try a pencil grip to make it easier. Pencil grips in different shapes, materials, and designs are available.

- Have students try a mechanical pencil if they frequently break pencil tips from applying too much pressure.

- Have students use erasable pens.

- Set realistic, mutually agreed-on expectations for neatness.

- Experiment with different kinds of paper. Some children find it easier to write when they use narrow-ruled paper (shorter line height); others do better using paper that is wide ruled.

- If a student's paper frequently slides around, attach the paper to a clipboard.

- Use writing tools other than paper and pencil, such as chalkboards with colored chalk or dry-erase boards with colored pens.

- Post your expectations for how assignments should appear (for example, writing on one side of the paper only, draft papers written on alternate lines, math papers with two or three line spaces between problems).

- Provide strips or charts of alphabet letters (manuscript or cursive) on students' desks for reference while they are forming letters. Draw directional arrows on letters that students find confusing to write.

- Provide visual cues such as starting dots and numbered arrows in order to support correct letter formation (direction and sequence of strokes).

Assistive Technology

- See Checklist 2.13 for information on assistive technology that is available and beneficial for students with dyslexia.

- Ensure that students receive the assistive technology (tools and training) designated in their IEP or 504 accommodation plan.

- Allow the use of text-to-speech software, word prediction software or devices, spelling checkers that speak word choices aloud, or other tools to help individuals with dyslexia bypass many roadblocks to writing. Technology allows access to printed material (by hearing it) that could not be accessed in the usual manner (reading it) and gives students the ability to produce written work that meets grade-level standards.

2.15 Games and Activities
to Strengthen Literacy and Language Skills

For children with dyslexia, learning to read involves systematic, intensive instruction. Additional practice in reading and language skills that is fun and outside of formal instruction helps children practice and improve these skills. Because multisensory learning is most effective, games and hands-on activities work well for reinforcing and expanding literacy skills. Many materials for use at school and home are available commercially. Activities that use handmade materials are inexpensive and provide children with fun ways to engage with concepts they have recently learned or need to review.

Online Literacy Games

- Adrian Bruce's free educational resources
  www.adrianbruce.com
- Harcourt School Publishers (On their Web site, enter "Learning Site"; search "reading" and "spelling" for activities.)
  www.harcourtschool.com
- BBC Words and Pictures
  www.bbc.co.uk/schools/wordsandpictures
- Starfall
  www.starfall.com
- Henderson Educational Software (word sorts for computers)
  www.HendersonEdSoft.com

Reading Games for Use at School or Home

- Dorbooks
  www.dorbooks.com

- Frog Publications
  www.frog.com
- EAI Education
  www.eaieducation.com
- ELGames.com, Next Generation Training, Inc.
  www.educationallearninggames.com

Reading and Spelling Manipulatives

- Really Good Stuff
  www.reallygoodstuff.com
- Crossbow Education
  www.crossboweducation.com
- Reading Manipulatives
  www.readskill.com

Additional online resources are listed at the end of this section.

Activities with Handmade Materials

Adapt commercial board games so that they provide reading or spelling practice. For example, make a duplicate set of cards that contains sight words or words with specific patterns (such as silent *e*). A child selects a card and reads the word or answers a question in order to move to the next space. The game can usually be played according to its original rules.

- Make bingo cards that can be used to reinforce newly learned skills. Here are some ways that bingo can be adapted:
  - Single words are written on the card. The caller reads a word. If a child can attach the word that was called to one on their card in order to make a compound word,

that space can be covered (for example, *snow-man*, *door-mat*).

- A child can cover a word on the card if it rhymes with the word being called.

- The caller says a word. If a child has the beginning letter (or, alternatively, the ending letter) of that word, that space can be covered.

- Words can be covered that are synonyms (mean the same) or antonyms (mean the opposite) as the word that is called.

- The meaning of a word is called out. Children can cover a word that has that definition.

- Create interlocking puzzle pieces. Children build words by connecting pieces that fit together. Create compound words, add prefixes and suffixes to root words, or match homophones (words that sound the same but are spelled differently). Words that rhyme or have the same word chunks (for example, *-un*, *-ack*) can also be used.

- Use magnetic letters to build words, sentences, or poems on a refrigerator or a metal board.

- Play games such as Hangman to reinforce spelling and reading skills.

- Select a letter. See how many words a child can think of that begin with that letter. This makes a good team game. For a more advanced game, have children think of as many words as they can that begin (or end) with a letter and fit into a specific category (for example, vegetables or clothing).

- Create cards for a memory game. Students turn over any two words and try to create a match. If a match is not made, they try to remember the location of the cards for a later turn. This game can be used to review sight words (create pairs of sight words), vocabulary words and definitions, rhyming words, antonyms, synonyms, homophones, or comprehension questions and answers.

Other Activities That Help Build Language Skills

Language and literacy skills involve many important components besides purely academic ones: memory, attention to detail, listening, motivation, effort, curiosity, and concentration. Building competence in these areas helps children to become better readers. Using games and play helps them improve language and literacy abilities while having fun. Including a variety of activities helps nurture an eagerness to learn, read, and explore. Encourage children to try the following:

- Working on puzzles and mazes
- Playing visual discrimination games (Which picture is different in this row? Which two cats are exactly the same? What is missing here?)
- Writing and performing short skits
- Making up poems and songs
- Visiting museums and historic places
- Reading children's magazines, riddle books, or sports news
- Following a shopping list
- Following a recipe
- Building a model, using directions
- Observing in nature
- Discussing interesting experiences
- Listening to stories
- Attending children's theater productions

See Checklists 2.1, 2.2, 2.3, 2.4, 2.5, 2.6, 2.8, 3.6 for more ideas on games and activities to build skills in phonological awareness, phonics, sight word recognition, spelling, and vocabulary.

2.16 The Basic Spelling Vocabulary List

This list, developed by Steven Graham, Karen Harris, and Connie Loynachan (2008), was devised to help educators know which spelling words should be taught to children. The list contains 850 words that account for 80 percent of the words children use in their writing—the ones they need to be able to spell correctly.

Grade 1

a	dad	home	of	six
all	day	hot	oh	so
am	did	I	old	stop
and	do	if	on	sun
at	dog	in	one	ten
ball	fat	into	out	the
be	for	is	pan	this
bed	fun	it	pet	to
big	get	its	pig	top
book	go	let	play	toy
box	good	like	ran	two
boy	got	look	rat	up
but	had	man	red	us
came	hat	may	ride	was
can	he	me	run	we
car	hen	mom	sat	will
cat	here	my	see	yes
come	him	no	she	you
cow	his	not	sit	

Used with permission of the *Journal of Educational Research*, 86(6), 363–368, July/ August 1993. Reprinted with permission of the Helen Dwight Reid Educational Foundation. Published by Heldref Publications, 1319 Eighteenth St., NW, Washington, DC 20036–1802. Copyright © 1993.

Grade 2

about	bus	eat	girl	jump
add	buy	eating	give	just
after	by	egg	glad	keep
ago	cake	end	goat	king
an	call	fall	goes	know
any	candy	far	going	lake
apple	change	farm	gold	land
are	child	fast	gone	last
as	city	father	grade	late
ask	clean	feed	grass	lay
ate	club	feel	green	left
away	coat	feet	grow	leg
baby	cold	fell	hand	light
back	coming	find	happy	line
bad	corn	fine	hard	little
bag	could	fire	has	live
base	cry	first	have	lives
bat	cup	fish	hear	long
bee	cut	five	help	looking
been	daddy	fix	here	lost
before	dear	flag	hill	lot
being	deep	floor	hit	love
best	deer	fly	hold	mad
bike	doing	food	hole	made
bill	doll	foot	hop	make
bird	door	four	hope	many
black	down	fox	horse	meat
blue	dress	from	house	men
boat	drive	full	how	met
both	drop	funny	ice	mile
bring	dry	game	inch	milk
brother	duck	gas	inside	mine
brown	each	gave	job	miss

moon	over	sea	take	walk
more	page	seat	talk	want
most	park	seem	tall	warm
mother	part	seen	teach	wash
move	pay	send	tell	way
much	pick	set	than	week
must	plant	seven	thank	well
myself	playing	sheep	that	went
nail	pony	ship	them	were
name	post	shoe	then	wet
need	pull	show	there	what
new	put	sick	they	when
next	rabbit	side	thing	while
nice	rain	sing	think	white
night	read	sky	three	who
nine	rest	sleep	time	why
north	riding	small	today	wind
now	road	snow	told	wish
nut	rock	some	too	with
off	room	soon	took	woke
only	said	spell	train	wood
open	same	start	tree	work
or	sang	stay	truck	yellow
other	saw	still	try	yet
our	say	store	use	your
outside	school	story	very	zoo

Grade 3

able	air	also	art	beach
above	airplane	always	aunt	bear
afraid	almost	animal	balloon	because
afternoon	alone	another	bark	become
again	along	anything	barn	began
age	already	around	basket	begin

behind	didn't	free	kind	nearly
believe	dinner	Friday	kitten	never
below	dishes	friend	knew	news
belt	does	front	knife	noise
better	done	getting	lady	nothing
birthday	don't	given	large	number
body	dragon	grand-	largest	o'clock
bones	draw	mother	later	often
born	dream	great	learn	oil
bought	drink	grew	leave	once
bread	early	ground	let's	orange
bright	earth	guess	letter	order
broke	east	hair	life	own
brought	eight	half	list	pair
busy	even	having	living	paint
cabin	ever	head	lovely	paper
cage	every	heard	loving	party
camp	everyone	he's	lunch	pass
can't	everything	heat	mail	past
care	eyes	hello	making	penny
carry	face	high	maybe	people
catch	family	himself	mean	person
cattle	feeling	hour	merry	picture
cave	felt	hundred	might	place
children	few	hurry	mind	plan
class	fight	hurt	money	plane
close	fishing	I'd	month	please
cloth	flower	I'll	morning	pocket
coal	flying	I'm	mouse	point
color	follow	inches	mouth	poor
corner	forest	isn't	Mr.	race
cotton	forgot	it's	Mrs.	reach
cover	form	I've	Ms.	reading
dark	found	kept	music	ready
desert	fourth	kids	near	real

rich	smoke	strong	tonight	wife
right	soap	study	trade	wild
river	someone	such	trick	win
rocket	something	sugar	trip	window
rode	sometime	summer	trying	winter
round	song	Sunday	turn	without
rule	sorry	supper	twelve	woman
running	sound	table	twenty	won
salt	south	taken	uncle	won't
says	space	taking	under	wool
sending	spelling	talking	upon	word
sent	spent	teacher	wagon	working
seventh	sport	team	wait	world
sew	spring	teeth	walking	would
shall	stairs	tenth	wasn't	write
short	stand	that's	watch	wrong
shot	state	their	water	yard
should	step	these	weather	year
sight	stick	thinking	we're	yesterday
sister	stood	third	west	you're
sitting	stopped	those	wheat	
sixth	stove	thought	where	
sled	street	throw	which	

Grade 4

across	build	cities	during	field
against	building	clothes	eighth	fifth
answer	built	company	else	finish
awhile	captain	couldn't	enjoy	following
between	carried	country	enough	good-by
board	caught	discover	everybody	group
bottom	charge	doctor	example	happened
breakfast	chicken	doesn't	except	harden
broken	circus	dollar	excuse	haven't

heavy	parent	return	threw	we'll
held	peanut	Saturday	tired	whole
hospital	pencil	scare	together	whose
idea	picnic	second	tomorrow	women
instead	police	since	toward	wouldn't
known	pretty	slowly	tried	writing
laugh	prize	stories	trouble	written
middle	quite	student	truly	wrote
minute	radio	sudden	turtle	yell
mountain	raise	suit	until	young
ninth	really	sure	village	
ocean	reason	swimming	visit	
office	remember	though	wear	

Grade 5

although	cousin	happiness	probably	surely
America	decide	important	problem	surprise
among	different	interest	receive	they're
arrive	evening	piece	sentence	through
attention	favorite	planet	several	usually
beautiful	finally	present	special	
countries	future	president	suddenly	
course	happiest	principal	suppose	

Resources

There are many resources for learning more about topics in this section. The following provide valuable information and useful strategies in the areas of reading, writing, and language.

Online Reading Resources

- Florida Center for Reading Research
  www.fcrr.org
- International Reading Association
  www.readingonline.org
- *Kindergarten and First Grade Student Center Activities, Book 1: Phonological Awareness and Phonics Student Center Activities*, published by the Florida Center for Reading Research, is available free for download.
  http://www.fcrr.org/Curriculum/studentCenterActivities.htm
- Phonics and Word Games
  http://www.adrianbruce.com/reading/games.htm
- Reading A-Z
  www.readinga-z.com
- Reading Rockets
  www.readingrockets.org
- The Reading Genie (site of Bruce Murray at Auburn University)
  http://www.auburn.edu/academic/education/reading_genie
- ReadWriteThink, a Web site based on a partnership between the International Reading Association and the National Council of Teachers of English
  http://www.readwritethink.org/student_mat/index.aspclassroom.
- University of Texas at Austin, Vaughn Gross Center for Reading and Language Arts
  www.texasreading.org

- Other Web sites related to reading, writing, and language information and supports are found in Sections One and Two.

Books, Articles, Programs, and Assessment Tools

Archer, A. L., Gleason, M. M., & Vachon, V. (2000). *REWARDS: Reading Excellence: Word Attack and Rate Development Strategies.* Longmont, CO: Sopris West Educational Services.

Auman, M. (2008). *Step up to writing.* Longmont, CO: Sopris West Educational Services.

Bear, D. R., Invernizzi, M., Templeton, S., & Johnston, F. (2004). *Words their way* (3rd ed.). Upper Saddle River, NJ: Pearson Education.

Bender, W. N., & Larkin, M. J. (2003). *Reading strategies for elementary students with learning difficulties.* Thousand Oaks, CA: Corwin Press.

Blachman, B. A., Ball, E. W., Black, R., & Tangel, D. M. (2000). *Road to the code: A phonological awareness program for young children.* Baltimore: Brookes.

Blevins, W. (2001). *Teaching phonics and word study in the intermediate grades: A complete sourcebook.* New York: Scholastic.

Ellis, E. (2004). *Makes Sense graphic organizers.* Northport, AL: Masterminds Publishing. www.graphicorganizers.com

Fetzer, N. (2003). *Writing connections: From oral language to written text.* Murrieta, CA: Nancy Fetzer's Literacy Connections.

Fetzer, N., & Rief, S. (2000). *Alphabet learning center activities kit.* San Francisco: Jossey-Bass.

Fry, E., and Kress, J. (2006). *The reading teacher's book of lists* (5th ed.). San Francisco: Jossey-Bass.

Ganske, K. (2000). *Word journeys: Assessment-guided phonics, spelling, and vocabulary instruction.* New York: Guilford Press.

Hall, S. L., & Moats, L. C. (2006). *Straight talk about reading.* New York: McGraw-Hill.

Harris, K. R., & Graham, S. (2005). *Writing better: Effective strategies for teaching students with learning difficulties.* Baltimore: Brookes.

Harris, K. R., Graham, S., Mason, L. H., Friedlander, B., & Reid, R. (2007). *Powerful writing strategies for all students.* Baltimore: Brookes.

Harvey, S., & Goudvis, A. (2007). *Strategies that work: Teaching comprehension for understanding and engagement.* York, ME: Stenhouse.

Hasbrouck, J., & Tindal, G. A. (2006). Oral reading fluency norms: A valuable assessment tool for reading teachers. *The Reading Teacher.* 59(7), 636–644.

Jager, M., Adams, B., Foorman, B., Lindbar, I., & Beeler, T. (1998). *Phonemic awareness in young children.* Baltimore: Brookes.

Kaminski, R. A., & Good, R. H. (1996). *DIBELS phoneme segmentation fluency.* Eugene, OR: University of Oregon. http://dibels.uoregon.edu/measures/psf.php

Klinger, J. K., Vaughn, S., Dimino, J., Schumm, J., & Bryant, D. (2001). *Collaborative strategic reading*. Longmont, CO: Sopris West Educational Services.

Mariconda, B., & Auray, D. P. (2005). *The comprehensive expository writing guide: All the skills you need to teach good writing* (2nd ed.). Trumbull, CT: Empowering Writers.

McKenna, M. C., & Stahl, S. A. (2003). *Assessment for reading instruction*. New York: Guilford Press.

Murray, B. (1999). *How to study spelling words*. Retrieved from the Web site The Reading Genie, Auburn University: http://www.auburn.edu/rdggenie/spelling.html

Notari-Syverson, A., O'Connor, R. E., & Vadasy, P. F. (2007). *Ladders to literacy*. Baltimore: Brookes.

Rasinski, T. (2003). *The fluent reader: Oral reading strategies for building word recognition, fluency, and comprehension*. New York: Scholastic.

Rief, S. (2005). *How to reach and teach children with ADD/ADHD* (2nd ed.). San Francisco: Jossey-Bass.

Rief, S. (2008). *The ADD/ADHD checklist: A practical reference for parents and teachers*. San Francisco: Jossey-Bass.

Rief, S., & Heimburge, J. (2007). *How to reach and teach all children through balanced literacy*. San Francisco: Jossey-Bass.

Schumaker, J. B., Denton, P. H., & Deshler, D. D. (1984). *The paraphrasing strategy*. Lawrence: University of Kansas.

Schumaker, J. B., Nolan, S. M., & Deshler, D. D. (1985). *Learning strategies curriculum: The error monitoring strategy*. Lawrence: University of Kansas Center for Research on Learning.

Throop, S. (1999). *Success with sight words: Multisensory ways to teach high-frequency words*. Huntington Beach, CA: Creative Teaching Press.

Torgesen, J. K., & Bryant, B. R. (1994). *Phonological awareness training for reading*. Austin, TX: Pro-Ed.

Townend, J., & Turner, M. (2000). *Dyslexia in practice: A guide for teachers*. New York: Kluwer Academic/Plenum.

Wilson, R. M., Hall, M., Leu, D. J., & Kinzer, C. K. (2001). *Phonics, phonemic awareness, and word analysis for teachers*. Columbus, OH: Merrill/Prentice Hall.

Yopp, H. K. (1995). Yopp-Singer test of phoneme segmentation. *The Reading Teacher, 49*(1), 20–29.

Vocabulary

- Merriam-Webster Online (dictionary)
  www.merriam-webster.com or www.m-w.com

- Online dictionary
  www.dictionary.com
- Online thesaurus
  www.thesaurus.com
- Online visual thesaurus
  www.visualthesaurus.com
- Online picture dictionary
  www.pdictionary.com
- Vocabulary University® (This Web site provides a wide variety of word lists, activities, puzzles, games, and vocabulary lesson plans for all grades.)
  www.vocabulary.com
- Games and activities for children at different levels
  www.funbrain.com/words.html
- Electronic dictionaries
  www.franklin.com/estore/dictionary

Software and Online Programs

There are various reading intervention programs (software and online) designed to build reading and other language-based skills. The following list includes programs that have a scientific research base and may be beneficial for children with dyslexia. Checklist 1.8, Research-Based Intervention Programs for Struggling Readers, includes more information on some of them.

- **AMP Reading System** (Pearson) is an intervention program for middle school and high school students who are reading at a third- to fifth-grade level. Available at www.pearsonschool.com
- **Headsprout® Early Reading** (Headsprout) teaches phonics and other reading fundamentals with an online curriculum

especially designed for students in kindergarten through second grade or older struggling readers. Available at www .headsprout.com

- **Intellitools Classroom Suite 4** (Intellitools) is an intervention program for reading and writing for students in preschool through fifth grade. Available at www.intellitools .com

- **Lexia Reading** (Lexia Learning) consists of interactive software programs that support reading skills development at all levels. Available at www.lexialearning.com

- **Read 180** (Scholastic) is an intensive reading intervention program that uses adaptive instructional software, high-interest literature, and direct instruction in reading, writing, and vocabulary skills. Available at www.teacher.scholastic.com

- **Reading Plus®** (Reading Plus) is a comprehensive assessment and instructional reading intervention program that addresses phonemic awareness, phonics, vocabulary, comprehension, and fluency. Available at www.readingplus .com

- **SuccessMaker® Reading** (SuccessMaker) teaches concepts and skills that address instructional needs within the five major components of reading for students in kindergarten through fifth grade. Available at www.pearsonschool.com

- **Waterford Early Reading Program** (Waterford Institute) is a comprehensive curriculum that teaches children how to read, write, and keyboard. Available at www.waterford.org

Online Writing Resources

- The Access Center Improving Outcomes for All Students K–8 http://www.k8accesscenter.org/training_resources/ languagearts.asp#Wbrief

- Essay Information
  http://essayinfo.com/essays
- Intervention Central
  www.interventioncentral.org
- The Writing Center, University of North Carolina at Chapel Hill
  http://www.unc.edu/depts/wcweb
- Writing Fix (interactive writing prompts)
  www.writingfix.com

Learning Strategies

Here are some sources of learning strategies to help students with dyslexia and other learning difficulties use metacognitive skills and self-regulated strategies during reading and writing:

- Self-regulated Strategy Development model, developed by Karen Harris, Steve Graham, and other researchers through the National Center on Accelerating Student Learning (CASL)
  http://kc.vanderbilt.edu/casl
- Strategy Instruction Model, developed at the Institute for Research in Learning Disabilities at the University of Kansas Center for Research on Learning
  www.ku-crl.org/sim
- Learning Toolbox Strategies, developed at James Madison University's Special Education Program
  http://coe.jmu.edu/learningtoolbox
- Cognitive Strategy Instruction, developed at the University of Nebraska–Lincoln
  http://www.unl.edu/csi/writing.shtml

Comprehensive Training Programs for Reading Teachers, Coaches, and Regular Classroom Teachers

- **LETRS (Language Essentials for Teachers of Reading and Spelling),** by Louisa C. Moats, provides twelve modules of training that address every component of effective reading instruction—phonological and phonemic awareness; phonics, decoding, spelling, and word study; oral language; vocabulary; reading fluency; comprehension; and writing—as well as the foundational concepts of language that link to all of these components. Available from Sopris West Educational Services, a Cambium Learning Company, at www.sopriswest.com or www.LETRS.com.

- **Teaching Reading Essentials,** by Louisa C. Moats and Linda Farrell, is a professional development program that demonstrates how to teach beginning reading to challenging students, using research-based strategies. Videos demonstrate small group reading interventions for students in kindergarten through third grade. Available from Sopris West Educational Services, a Cambium Learning Company, at www.sopriswest.com/tre.

3

CHECKLISTS FOR PARENTS

Introduction

Parents are an essential part of the educational team that works with children who have dyslexia. They advocate for their child's learning needs, help with reading at home, find outside services when needed, and provide ongoing encouragement to a child who often finds learning discouraging. Parenting a child with dyslexia is not an easy job, so knowing where to look for help, ideas, and information is important.

3.1 Talking with Your Child About Dyslexia and Other Learning Differences

Helping children understand their own learning profile is an important part of any intervention process. At an early age, children begin to compare themselves with their peers. As school life becomes more difficult for a student with dyslexia, blame, frustration, embarrassment, and decreased motivation can become damaging by-products. In contrast, when a child understands the nature of his or her learning problems, there is a greater likelihood of seeing them as part of the big picture—areas of weakness among many strengths, as well as a difficulty that has a name and can be dealt with successfully.

Young children, adolescents, and young adults with dyslexia should all be part of these conversations about how to help them succeed. As they mature in their language and cognitive skills, they become able to understand the increasingly more complex concepts involved in understanding dyslexia and other learning disorders.

While some parents and teachers are concerned about the idea of labeling a child, using terms such as *dyslexia* and *learning disability* are much less cruel and inaccurate than words used by children themselves (*dumb, slow, lazy*). This is how children might think of themselves if they have never participated in discussions meant to describe their difficulties in straightforward, respectful ways.

How and When to Bring Up the Topic of Dyslexia

- When children begin to ask questions. ("Why is everyone in the class reading a harder book than I am?" "Why do I have to go to a tutor every week?")
- When children begin to express frustration or anger about their learning problems.
- When children have academic success. Talk about why something went well (taking a test with extended time, using a different study technique).

- When teachable moments arise. Explain difficulties and make suggestions to help overcome them. ("Let's look at the hard words on the page before you start reading, so you can figure them out. Would you like to try reading the chapter in two parts, so you can take a short break in between?")
- When famous people with dyslexia are discussed in the media. Point out their success, especially when their hard work paid off.
- When reassurance is needed. Discuss with the child that the members of the child's support team want to help him or her and the ways that they can help. If a child needs extra time to copy an assignment or an opportunity to get additional explanations for an assignment, a specific person may be designated as the "go-to person." It is helpful for a child to know who is available for different kinds of problems that may be encountered.

What Should Be Included in a Discussion
- Reassure children about their intelligence, which is one of the criteria for the diagnosis of dyslexia.
- Let children know that there are many children, teens, and adults with dyslexia in the United States and around the world.
- Talk about how everyone has strengths and weaknesses, using yourself as a model. ("At work, I am the best person at planning events, but I always need help with using my computer.")
- Point out your child's strengths, and show that you value them.
- Provide children with self-respectful words to use when a sibling or friend asks a question, such as why they go to a special class or school. In this case, having a child explain in a matter-of-fact way that he or she is getting extra help in writing or organization skills usually is sufficient.

- Discuss the specific features of a child's difficulty (for example, sounding out words, reading slowly, spelling words).

- Provide suggestions for self-talk. When a child struggles with homework, words like "This is hard for me, but I will get it done" or "I know who can help me with this if I need it" create a more positive approach to a potential problem.

- Discuss ideas with the child about ways to address concerns. Children, parents, teachers, and counselors can all initiate these kind of conversations.

Issues to Take into Consideration

- Consider the child's vocabulary and cognitive skills when talking about learning problems. Young children will be ready for less information than an adolescent who has had these discussions before.

- Make sure that the child understands that a learning disability should not be used as an excuse later. The focus should be on explaining the difficulties so that ways to manage them can be figured out.

- Avoid lecturing. Short, clear messages work best.

- Build on information that a child has already learned or heard from others (such as teachers).

- Be honest. Telling a child that work is easy and that he or she can do it just like everyone else is not a fair assessment of the situation.

- Convey the message that having dyslexia doesn't limit the child's potential, that with help and hard work the child can achieve his or her goals. Let the child know that there are highly successful adults with dyslexia in every profession and walk of life.

- Consider letting other people in the child's life know about ways to help. (For example, a soccer coach will benefit from knowing about a child's difficulty with oral directions, and a Sunday school teacher may need to know about a child's reading and writing difficulties.)

- Encourage your child to let teachers and other adults know what is helpful. ("Please don't ask me to read out loud in front of the class." "When you give directions out loud, could you also write them down?")

- Encourage questions and open communication about the problems your child is struggling with and how to address those challenges. Children should also be encouraged to come up with their own suggestions, so that they learn to solve problems.

Resources for Children

Books provide an opportunity for children with dyslexia to learn more about themselves from someone outside of their own world. This list includes fiction and nonfiction works. The books can be read independently or together with an adult, depending on the child's reading skills. These books are good sources of questions, discussion points, and means to clear up misperceptions.

Betancourt, J. (1993). *My name is Brain Brian*. New York: Scholastic.

Cummings, R., & Fisher, G. (2002). *The survival guide for kids with LD: Learning differences*. Minneapolis, MN: Free Spirit.

Lawton, S. (Ed.). (2005). *Learning disabilities information for teens*. Detroit: Omnigraphics.

Moore-Mallinos, J. (2007). *It's called dyslexia*. Hauppauge, NY: Barron's Educational Series.

Paquette, P. (2006). *Learning disabilities: The ultimate teen guide*. Metuchen, NJ: Scarecrow Press.

Robb, D. (2004). The alphabet war: A story about dyslexia. Morton Grove, IL: Whitman.

Stern, J., & Ben-Ami, U. (1996). *Many ways to learn: Young people's guide to learning disabilities*. Washington, DC: Magination Press.

3.2 How to Advocate for Your Child

Parents of children with dyslexia frequently have no training in advocating for their children's needs, yet it is a role they must often play in the educational setting. Advocating for a child may involve an understanding of effective informal means as well as legal procedures.

Becoming familiar with children's educational rights, learning to communicate well, and holding firm when necessary allow parents to be a significant part of the team that works to meet a child's needs. Combining tact, knowledge, and persistence can go a long way in creating a productive relationship with a child's school community.

Keep Up with Your Own Homework

- Use a notebook to keep important documents (such as copies of evaluations, work papers, and past meeting notes). This practice will provide easy access to information at meetings, as well as a good record to share when a child makes a transition to a new school or when you are consulting with an outside professional.

- Become familiar with federal and state standards for an appropriate education for a child with a disability.

  - By law, children are entitled to a free appropriate public education.

  - The Individuals with Disabilities Education Act (IDEA) outlines due process that must be followed in order to determine a child's eligibility for special education programs, as well as procedures that must be followed by the school system. (See Checklist 5.4.)

  - If parents or school districts disagree with special education decisions, they may request a due process hearing. This hearing is conducted by an impartial hearing officer. Parents may choose to represent themselves or hire an attorney.

- See Checklists 5.4, 5.5, and 5.6 for more on federal educational rights of children with disabilities.

- Understand the results of your child's testing. If necessary, seek out someone to explain the results, so you have a clear idea of your child's strengths and weaknesses, as well as recommendations for how to help him or her succeed. (See Checklist 1.7.)

- Learn about your child's disability through reading, discussions with professionals and parents, and attendance at conferences. Knowledge in the field of dyslexia and disability rights frequently changes; staying informed allows you to increase your knowledge and use it to your child's advantage.

- Be wary of new ideas and products that promise to cure dyslexia, so that your requests to the school are reasonable. Research-based methods and materials used by trained, knowledgeable professionals are considered the most effective means of helping a child with dyslexia.

- Know the goals on your child's IEP, so that you can follow up in making sure that they are being worked on.

- Although private and parochial schools are not obligated to provide the same services as public schools, advocating for your child's needs is still important. Meeting with teachers and school staff, providing information obtained from outside professionals, and keeping lines of communication open are all effective ways to make sure your child benefits in his or her school environment.

Use Positive Communication

- Sometimes there is a fine line between being a steady advocate and being a pest. Ask for what is appropriate. Avoid demands that may be unreasonable. Choose words carefully and avoid antagonism. Many requests can be framed in such a way that they invite discussion rather than refusal.

- Create a good working relationship. Try to see yourself as part of the team. You are asking your child's teachers and school to go the extra mile for your child. Offer your own help and cooperation. It's not only about the letter of the law.

- Remember that the law may ensure that requirements are met, but your tone and manner can help create a strong, positive relationship or an adversarial one with a school. Staff members are more likely to work with you when they feel supported and appreciated.

- Communicate with teachers early in the year. Try to keep this up during the school year.

- Get to know the guidance counselor and learning specialists at your child's school. Establish a comfortable means of informal communication so that you can receive information regularly.

- Use communication tools provided by the school (homework hot lines, grades posted online, teachers' Web sites, and e-mail).

- Keep a record of your attempts to reach school or district staff members. If you are unable to get through to someone in a timely manner, contact the supervisor.

- Keep in mind that your child is one student in the school. Monitor the way you may be coming across. Would you talk to a doctor or accountant that way?

- Listen carefully to what teachers have to say. They are often real advocates for your child. If not, maintaining positive communication and providing helpful information may establish a better working relationship.

Learn How to Handle Meetings Effectively

Formal team meetings are held in schools in order to discuss student referrals for testing, eligibility for special education services, monitoring of educational progress, and formulation or review of Individualized Education Programs (IEPs). See Checklist 5.5. Different states use different terms to refer to these meetings. The meetings may include the classroom teacher(s), special education teacher, other learning or reading specialists, learning and reading specialists, a counselor, a speech-language pathologist, a school psychologist, a social worker, and an administrator. Parents are invited to these meetings by written communication.

- Prepare your own notes ahead of time. If there are specific issues you would like to discuss, write them down so that you can be sure to cover them during the meeting.
- Don't be intimidated by professional jargon. If you are unsure about what a term or acronym means, ask for an explanation.
- Speak up if you feel that your point of view has not been heard. Be open to what the other team members have to say, but make sure that your concerns are expressed as well.
- Take your own notes at meetings. Compare them with the copy that is provided by the school.
- If you are uncomfortable or overwhelmed by the process of appearing at a meeting by yourself, attend the meeting with another person such as a spouse, a family member, or an advocate.

Know When You Need Additional Support or Services

- Hiring a private consultant to provide an evaluation of your child's learning needs is an important step if your child does not qualify for an evaluation through the school system or if you believe more information is needed. Clinics, hospitals, and private evaluators in your area should be considered if you decide to have a private evaluation.
- If your child is working privately with a tutor, educational therapist, speech-language pathologist, or mental health

professional, you may want to bring that person to the school to participate in meetings with a consultant or with the school team.

- Special education advocates and educational consultants who have worked with you regarding your child may also be helpful supports during a meeting.

- You may want to consider hiring a legal advocate who specializes in education law if you have had a history of difficulty in dealing with the school or district or if you believe that your child is not receiving the educational services to which he or she is entitled.

3.3 Finding a Tutor or Educational Therapist

Tutors, educational therapists, and academic language therapists can be very helpful to students with dyslexia. They are able to use teaching methods that are geared to the needs of a specific child. The pace and type of instruction can be adapted to the child, and immediate feedback and reinforcement can be provided.

Educational therapists are teachers who are trained and certified to work individually with students who have academic and learning disabilities. They can be found in some parts of the country. For further information on the National Association of Educational Therapists, see http://www.aetonline.org.

Academic language therapists work with students who have a variety of difficulties, such as dyslexia and written language disorders. They are trained to work with students in various areas of reading. For further information, see http://www.altaread.org.

While not every student with dyslexia needs to work with a private tutor, educational therapist, or academic language therapist, parents may want to explore this option at different times during a child's school years. Knowing what to look for makes the search easier.

Determining Whether a Child Needs a Tutor or Educational Therapist

- Talk with people at the school who know your child: the classroom teacher, the special education teacher or learning specialist, and the counselor. Obtain their opinions about getting extra academic help for your child.
- Parents should be honest with themselves. Ask questions such as these:
  - Has helping with homework become a nightly battle? Does it create tension between you and your child?

- Are you spending too much time with your child with dyslexia and insufficient time with your other children?
- Does your older child need help in subject areas (chemistry, algebra) that you are unable to provide?
- If your child has reading problems, does he or she need more intervention than the school provides during the day?
- Does your child become easily distracted when working in a group at school, thereby missing important instruction?

- Give an older child a say in the matter. Discuss with him or her some of the benefits of working with a tutor. Set up an introductory session to see whether your child feels comfortable with the tutor. Present tutoring as a positive option rather than as punishment.

- Avoid scheduling tutoring during times that conflict with activities that are important to the child (for example, Girl Scouts or soccer practice).

Locating the Right Person

- Decide what level of expertise you need. While some students benefit from working with an older student to help them with homework, students with dyslexia who need work on reading and writing skills should work with teachers who are experienced in teaching these subjects.

- Large commercial tutoring services do not always employ people who are trained and experienced in working with students with dyslexia. Check for a specific tutor's credentials rather than the reputation of the business.

- An effective tutor should have experience in using more than one method of reading instruction with students who have dyslexia. Because no one system works for everyone, and many children benefit from a combination of strategies, look for these qualifications.

- Check with your child's special education teacher or guidance counselor for names of recommended tutors.

- When interviewing potential tutors, ask them to describe their background and training. Ask questions about the methods, curriculum, and research-validated approaches they use and about their expertise in teaching students with reading disabilities.

- Check with local chapters of organizations such as the Learning Disabilities Association (LDA) that maintain a list of professionally certified tutors in the community.

- Go to the Web site of the International Dyslexia Association at www.interdys.org, and click on the link "Find a Provider."

- For names of Orton-Gillingham certified instructors, visit www.ortonacademy.org or www.dys-add.com.

- Check with private schools for children with learning disabilities in your community to see whether they have a tutoring service.

- Ask the tutors you are considering to provide you with references.

- Consider summer tutoring, when finding a qualified special education teacher or reading specialist may be easier.

- Look for personality characteristics that are important for your child, such as a sense of humor or predictability. Rapport between a tutor and a student is very important.

- Define your expectations for tutoring goals. Listen to the goals proposed by the tutor. Try to develop a level of trust and understanding early in the relationship. Good communication and respect help the process.

Making Effective Use of a Tutor

- Help the tutor develop a regular communication system with teachers and parents. E-mail or phone contact will help keep everyone "in the loop." Teachers will have an easier time this way sharing information on what the student is learning and what help is needed.

- Share information from any testing that has been done as well as the student's IEP, so that the tutor can develop individualized goals or support the child in meeting his or her IEP goals.

- Schedule sessions during times when your child is relaxed and able to focus well. Meeting with a tutor right after school might not work for a child who needs a break from a long academic day and time to relax or play.

- Encourage your child to identify work that is difficult in school and share it with the tutor, so that part of the session can be devoted to what the child has defined as a problem.

- Set up periodic separate meetings with the tutor to discuss concerns and questions about your child's progress. Avoid rushed meetings on these issues that interfere with the scheduled tutoring session.

3.4 Building and Nurturing Your Child's Self-Esteem

Children with dyslexia as well as other learning disabilities or ADHD may have fragile self-esteem. Experiencing frustration, lack of success, embarrassment, and negative feedback from others can take a heavy toll on a child's self-image, especially when he or she is doing the best he or she can.

Parents and teachers must understand that there are emotional burdens that often accompany a learning disability or ADHD and how to help children express those emotions. Parents must also take steps to enable their child to experience a healthy dose of success in other areas in order to build self-esteem.

Emotional Factors and Coping Mechanisms

Living with a learning disability can be very stressful and can make school a painful place to be. This disability can lead to feelings of inadequacy, low self-esteem, and to anxiety and depression, all of which may be expressed in various ways:

- To avoid embarrassment or failure because of their reading, writing, or other learning difficulties, children may
  - Feign illness in order to escape the situation
  - Misbehave in order to be sent out of the classroom
  - Hide schoolwork or "lose" it
  - Make up excuses not to perform a task
  - Display other avoidance behaviors
- Some children act up behaviorally as a coping mechanism. They would rather be labeled the class clown or bad instead of looking dumb.
- Children may have social problems as well as learning difficulties. Rejection and teasing may affect their self-esteem. Children with poor social skills may receive a lot of negative

feedback from adults (reprimands, criticism). To cope, they may

- Play with younger children rather than those in their own age group
- Gravitate toward others who do poorly in school
- Avoid activities that require interacting with other children
- Pretend that they don't care

- Many children exhibit anger and say or do things that aren't meant to harm others but are expressions of their frustration and hurt.
- Depression may appear as anger, as well as withdrawal and lack of energy.
- Low self-esteem may cause children to be hard on themselves or be self-deprecating—calling themselves "stupid" or seeing their flaws and not their assets.

How Children Acquire Self-Esteem

Children's self-esteem is built and shaped by

- Experiencing
  - Pride in their own accomplishments
  - Success in mastering skills and goals
  - The opportunity to pursue their interests, passions, and dreams
- Receiving
  - Positive feedback from significant others
  - Sincere praise and recognition for successes
  - Unconditional love, support, and belief from parents and others

- Feeling
  - Capable and competent (at least in some areas)
  - Liked, valued, and respected
  - That they have specific strengths and assets
  - Optimistic about the future
  - Positive about themselves

Strategies for Building Self-Esteem

- Help your child identify and recognize his or her talents, abilities, and positive traits.
- Help your child cultivate interests and develop areas of strength.
- Encourage and support participation in extracurricular activities such as clubs, sports, theater, or scouts.
- Ask teachers to enable your child to showcase his or her strengths and talents at school. Classmates typically know your child's areas of weakness but may be unaware of his or her strengths.
- Give your child reasonable, developmentally appropriate responsibilities to help develop self-confidence.
- Help your child set realistic mini-goals in order to take steps toward achieving bigger goals.
- When correcting your child, avoid sarcasm or criticism of his or her character or intelligence. When they misbehave, let children know that the behavior is inappropriate, not them. Let them know you are disappointed because you know they can do better.
- Let your children know that you appreciate them for who they are.
- Communicate unconditional love and unwavering belief in your child.

- Provide the help your child needs to build skills and competencies in areas of weakness. Be your child's strongest advocate and support.

- Display and save your child's projects or work that he or she is proud of. Maintain a portfolio collection of valued projects, or take photos of them to keep as a memory.

- Encourage your son or daughter to share experiences and feelings with you. Ask questions and take time to really listen. Show empathy, encouragement, and support.

- Teach your child strategies for dealing with negative emotions, such as positive self-talk ("I can do this. It's just a setback; I'll get past this.") or stress reduction and anger management (taking deep breaths or counting to ten before responding, visualizing something positive). A counselor or other professional can help teach such techniques.

- Be open and honest in discussing your child's reading disorder. Discuss how, in spite of the obstacles and having to work harder than others, he or she can be successful. (See Checklist 3.1.)

- Name and talk about the many successful people who have dyslexia or other learning disabilities. Share examples of famous people who bounced back from setbacks or had earlier failures before they succeeded. For example, Einstein flunked grade-school mathematics, and Walt Disney went bankrupt five times before he built Disneyland.

- Work with your child on problem-solving skills.

- Seek professional help if your child is not coping well emotionally, particularly if you suspect that your child is depressed or anxious.

3.5 How to Help Your Child with Homework

Homework time is often very stressful in homes of children with dyslexia and other learning disabilities. After a full day of school, having to work on and complete more assignments—particularly those involving reading and writing—is very difficult and frustrating for the child and the parents. To support your child through the homework process, consider these tips.

Creating a Work Environment

- Together with your child, establish one or two locations for doing homework—preferably, quiet work areas with adequate lighting.

- Limit distractions (unnecessary noise, activity, and phone calls) in your home during homework hours. Consider turning off the TV during homework time.

- Be sure that your child has the necessary supplies and an organized work space. (See Checklist 3.7.)

Homework Routine and Schedule

- Work out a schedule with your child—a specific time for homework each day. Adhere to the schedule as closely and consistently as possible in order to develop a homework habit.

- Consider a variety of factors when scheduling homework: extracurricular activities, mealtimes and bedtimes, chores and other responsibilities, your availability to supervise or monitor, and your child's preferences and learning styles.

- Some children prefer to start their homework shortly after they come home from school. Others need time to play and relax before they start their homework. However, it is recommended that the child not wait until the evening to get started.

- Some children prefer to do the easiest tasks or assignments first; others like to tackle the hardest ones first. Have your child try each way to find what works best.

- Encourage your child to get in the habit of putting all books, notebooks, signed notes, and other necessary materials inside his or her backpack before bedtime.

- Place your child's backpack in a consistent location so that he or she cannot miss seeing or tripping over it when leaving the house in the morning.

Preparation and Structuring

- Expect your child to record all assignments. Request the teacher's help in making sure that all assignments are recorded daily. Perhaps the teacher can initial or sign the student's planner or assignment sheet each day.

- Follow through by reviewing the recorded assignments with your child.

- Assist your child in dividing assignments into smaller segments that are more manageable and less overwhelming.

- Emphasize to your child the importance of not leaving school until he or she has double-checked the assignment sheet or planner and made sure that his or her backpack is loaded with all the books and materials needed to do the homework. Request such assistance from the teacher.

- Have your child obtain the phone numbers of a few responsible students whom he or she can call with questions about schoolwork.

- Find out whether your child's school has a homework hot line or whether teachers record assignments on their voicemail or post them on a class Web site.

- Help your child to first look over all homework assignments for the evening and then organize the materials needed before beginning homework.

- If your child frequently forgets to bring home textbooks, ask whether you can borrow another set for home use. If not, consider purchasing your own set.

- Assist your child with structuring long-range homework assignments such as reports and projects. Be vigilant in monitoring and supporting your child through this process. See Checklist 3.7 for more on this topic.

Help During Homework

- The amount of direct assistance required by your child during homework will depend on the complexity of the assignments, the reading and writing required, and the needs of your child.

- Assist your child in getting started on assignments (reading the directions and difficult words together; highlighting key words in the directions; doing the first few items together, then observing as your child does the next few problems or items independently). Then leave the room, if possible.

- Monitor and give feedback without doing all the work with your child. You want your child to attempt work independently.

- Allow breaks between homework assignments. Your child can reward himself or herself (with a snack, a play or exercise break, or time to call friends) after completing an assignment or two.

- Do not force your child to spend an excessive amount of time on homework. If you feel that your child has worked enough, write a note to the teacher indicating this and attach it to the homework.

- If your child struggles with writing, a common accommodation is to have the child dictate while you or someone else writes down what he or she says.

- It is not your responsibility or is it advisable to correct all of your child's errors on homework or make sure that papers are perfect.
- When homework time drags on, do not do the work for your child. Set a stop time. If the situation continues, have a discussion with the teacher (see the subsection "Communicate with Teachers About Homework Issues" later in this section).
- Provide encouragement and praise your child's effort.

Increasing Motivation and Work Production

Your child may need extra incentives (particularly if he or she also has ADHD). Try these suggestions:

- Use a kitchen timer to challenge your child to stay on task, and reward work completed with relative accuracy during that time frame. Tell your child that you will come back to check his or her progress on homework when the timer rings.
- Challenge your child to beat the clock. Such a challenge is often effective in motivating children to complete a task before the timer goes off.
- Help your child set up mini-goals of work completion (read x number of pages, finish writing one paragraph, complete a row of problems). After accomplishing the goal, the child can be rewarded with a break or points, tokens, or other reinforcers.
- Enforce consequences such as a loss of points on a token economy/behavior modification system when your child fails to bring home needed assignments or materials.
- Withhold privileges (TV or other screen time, access to phone) until a reasonable amount of homework has been completed.
- Supervise your child in placing completed work in his or her notebook or backpack to bring to school. Students with

memory and attention problems often forget to turn in their homework, even if they spent hours completing it. You may want to arrange with the teacher a system of collecting your child's homework immediately upon his or her arrival at school to ensure that your child turns in the work and receives credit for doing so.

Communicate with Teachers About Homework Issues

- If homework is a frequent cause of battles and frustration in your home, seek help. Make an appointment with your child's teacher to discuss homework problems, and request reasonable modifications and adjustments.

- Let teachers know the amount of time your child is taking and describe the stress your child is experiencing over homework. Explain the efforts you are making to help at home and through any tutorial help or services received outside of school.

- Let teachers know that you want to be frequently informed about how your child is keeping up with assignments. Work out an arrangement for communication, such as a weekly report or e-mail message.

Other Ways That Parents Can Help

- If homework accommodations and modifications are needed, be sure they are written into your child's Individualized Education Program (IEP). (See Checklist 5.5.)

- Help your child study for tests. Practice using a variety of multisensory formats and techniques. (See Checklists 2.8, 3.8, and 4.7.)

- Many parents find it very difficult to help their own child with schoolwork. If that is the case, find someone else who can help. Consider hiring a tutor. Often, a high school student or even a middle school student is ideal for providing assistance with daily homework, depending on the age of your child. However, for building reading or other academic skills, a well-qualified specialist will be needed. (See Checklist 3.3.)

- Consider purchasing or obtaining assistive technology that will support your dyslexic child in reading and writing independently. (See Checklist 2.13.)

3.6 Reinforcing Reading Skills at Home

Interest and involvement in reading should not stop when children leave school. Parents can reinforce important reading skills at home in positive, fun ways. The more children with dyslexia are engaged in reading activities, the more opportunities they will have to solidify their skills.

Helping Early Readers

- Play games together that involve the use of phonological awareness skills (see Checklist 2.1).
- Expose children to rhyme (poetry, music).
- Read and discuss books together.
- Play games that require early reading and spelling skills (board games, making words with manipulatives such as magnetic letters or alphabet stamps).
- Encourage children to read signs and brand names that they recognize.
- Have children listen to recorded stories and books, to nurture an interest in literature.
- Introduce new vocabulary words as they appear in books, in movies, in conversations, and during museum trips and other outings.
- Use activities that require sequencing skills: putting things in order from left to right, from beginning to end, in numerical or alphabetical order.

Helping Elementary School Readers

- Play word games. See Checklist 2.15.
- Continue to read to your child in order to build an appreciation of literature and model fluency skills.
  - Model the use of good expression.

- Discuss interesting aspects of the book you are reading with your child.

- Ask your child's opinion about parts of the book. Discuss characters and alternative solutions to problems in the book. Compare characters in different books, books to other books, or events in books with his or her own experiences.

- Encourage your child to read orally, if he or she is comfortable doing so. Children may be willing to read every other page or paragraph out loud, while parents read the others. Provide help with some of the words in order to keep the story moving along. Occasionally, have the child figure out new words by breaking them into syllables, dividing words into root words and affixes (prefixes or suffixes), or pointing out that the new word rhymes with another word they might know (for example *sound*, *ground*). See Checklist 2.3 for more ideas on helping your child with learning new words.

- Enjoy the use of interesting and descriptive words in literature. Look at dialogue. Read poetry together.

- Read children's plays together as a family, dividing up parts.

- Be sensitive to how your child feels when reading books that are easier than those read by younger siblings or by peers. Be positive and reassuring, so that reading does not become equated with embarrassment.

- Be gently persistent when encouraging your child to try something new or continuing when something feels difficult. Children with dyslexia may be hesitant to read books independently because they may not be fluent enough to enjoy the process. It may take greater involvement on a parent's part to help nurture an interest in leisure reading.

- Find a children's librarian who can talk with your child in order to find out what topics he or she finds interesting or books that he or she has enjoyed in the past, so that other books can be recommended.

- Check with your child's teacher, reading teacher, or librarian for suggestions on appropriate books for your child. A variety of high-interest books with easy vocabulary that may be engaging for struggling readers are available.

- While your child is getting comfortable with the reading process, encourage reading that involves specific interests. Reading sports pages, fashion magazines, or directions for putting together a model may motivate a child to read more than a book that holds no particular appeal.

- Monitor the amount of time that your child spends on watching television and playing on a computer. To become a proficient reader, plenty of reading practice is necessary. Decide on a reasonable amount of daily reading time. Provide interesting reading material and make it part of the daily schedule.

Helping Middle School and High School Readers

- Subscribe to magazines that interest your child.

- Discuss current events with your child. Point out articles on topics that your child wants to know more about.

- Recommend that your child keep a journal on a specific event or activity (a family trip, volunteer work, or nature observations).

- Encourage a reluctant reader to listen to audio books (fiction and nonfiction).

- Help your child plan reading times as part of his or her overall weekly schedule.

- Preview difficult words together before your child begins a book chapter for an assignment.

- Use your child's interests to introduce various types of reading (for example, cookbooks, car manuals, or instructions for installing software or doing a craft). Offer to go over information together so that your child will be more comfortable when he or she uses it independently.

- Model sophisticated vocabulary in your own language, to increase your child's exposure to new words.

Keeping Up Reading Skills During the Summer

A long summer vacation provides a needed respite for most students, but it may also result in their losing some of what they have learned during the previous school year. For students with dyslexia, it may be especially important to maintain and build reading skills during the summer. Avoid a summer slide by providing reading practice over the summer months. By continuing to practice reading, struggling readers will be less likely to start the school year at a disadvantage due to a lack of skill reinforcement. Consider some of the following suggestions:

- Enroll your child in a summer reading program that provides specialized small-group instruction.

- Consider tutoring sessions or educational therapy or academic language therapy for children who lag behind in reading skills. See Checklist 3.3.

- Check out summer library programs that reinforce leisure reading.

- Establish a regular reading schedule during the summer, taking into consideration your child's other activities.

- Ask your child's classroom teacher, learning specialist, or reading teacher for materials that can be used during the summer to reinforce reading skills.

Summer Reading and Learning Resources for Children

- American Library Association
  www.ala.org/ala/mgrps/divs/alsc/alscresources/summerread-ing/recsummerreading/recommendedreading.cfm
- Colorín Colorado (a bilingual site for families and educators of English language learners)
  www.colorincolorado.org/families/letsread/summer
- National Center for Family Literacy
  www.famlit.org
- National Geographic Kids
  http://kids.nationalgeographic.com
- PBS Kids: Between the Lions
  www.pbskids.org/lions
- Reading Is Fundamental
  www.rif.org/parents/tips
- Spark Top (activities for children with learning disabilities)
  www.SparkTop.org
- U.S. Department of Education
  www.ed.gov/parents/read/resources/edpicks.jhtml

3.7 Helping Your Child with Organization and Time Management

Poor organization and time management are common problems for children with learning disabilities. Fortunately, there are many ways to help strengthen these skills for your child's school success.

Strategies and Supports for Organization

Provide your child with support organizing items such as school and homework supplies and materials, as well as creating an organized work environment at home.

Supplies and Materials

- Provide your child with a backpack and a notebook or binder according to the teacher's specifications. By third or fourth grade, students often benefit from using a three-ring binder with colored subject dividers and a plastic pouch for pencils and other small supplies. Students in kindergarten through second grade can use a soft pocket folder for homework and other papers.

- Provide a spelling dictionary or a list of frequently misspelled words, a multiplication chart, and other useful reference materials for your child's notebook or binder.

- Insert a plastic sleeve into the binder for storing important papers that are not three-hole-punched.

- Place hole-punched colored folders in the binder—for example, red for homework, blue for parent notices or papers to be left at home. When folders are attached to notebook rings, papers that are placed in the folders have less chance of being lost or falling out.

- Include large laminated envelopes that are hole-punched in the binder, for homework, flash cards, or project papers.

- Use an accordion folder as an alternative to a three-ring binder if your child finds it easier to manage at school. The tabs of the accordion folder can be labeled for homework and each subject (preferably, according to the sequence of the student's schedule). Papers can be quickly placed behind the tab for that subject during the school day and refiled into a binder at home.

- Hole-punch your child's planner, monthly calendar, or assignment sheet and keep it in the front of the binder (or in the front or back of the accordion folder).

- Provide supplies to help your child stay organized at school. Have your child regularly take inventory of what needs replacement, or ask the teacher.

- Use a specific bag for organizing and holding supplies for your child's extracurricular activities. Provide a list inside a transparent plastic sleeve that itemizes what needs to be inside the bag (for example, equipment, shoes, uniform, or notebooks).

The Homework Supply Kit

- Reduce wasted time searching the house for homework supplies and materials by keeping them together in one place.

- Consider creating a portable homework supply kit in a lightweight container with a lid. With this system, it does not matter where your son or daughter chooses to study; the necessary supplies can accompany your child anywhere.

- Recommended supplies (depending on your child's age) include the following:

Plenty of paper	Paper clips
Sharpened pencils with erasers	Stapler and staples
Pencil sharpener	Three-hole punch
Ruler	Calculator

Crayons	Thesaurus
Paper hole reinforcers	Electronic spelling checker
Glue stick	Sticky notes
Colored pencils, pens, and markers	Highlighters
Clipboard	Index cards

Work Area

- Carefully examine your child's work space. Make sure there is a large working surface (desktop) that is free from clutter.
- Help your child clear out desk drawers and shelves. Together, decide what to keep and store (in colored boxes, portfolios, or large plastic zipped bags) in order to make room for current papers and projects.
- Provide your child with a corkboard and pins to hang up important papers.
- Provide storage space in order to organize your child's room efficiently: shelves, closet space, bins, drawers.
- Label shelves and storage bins.
- Keep a three-hole punch and electric pencil sharpener easily accessible.
- Provide your child with a desk or wall calendar (separate from the master family calendar), to help him or her maintain an overview of important dates, activities, and events. Older students may prefer to use electronic devices to record dates.

Visual Reminders and Organizational Cues

- Hang dry-erase boards in a central location of your home for phone messages and notes. Hang one in your child's room for important reminders and messages.
- Encourage your child to write reminders on colored sticky notes and place them on mirrors, doors, and other places where they are likely to be noticed.

- Use color strategically:
  - Provide a file with color-coded folders in which your child can keep papers stored categorically.
  - Color coordinate by subject—for example, green for the history notebook and history textbook cover, a schedule with the time and room number of the history class highlighted in green, and a green tab for the history subject divider in the notebook.
  - Color code entries on a calendar according to category (for example, school, sports, social activities).

More Organizational Tips

- Set a regular time to help your child organize his or her backpack, notebook, desk, and room. Help with sorting and discarding.
- Burn CDs of important schoolwork files, including digital pictures of school projects, to store on the computer for safekeeping.
- Set up a file box or drawer with files for each subject in which to store returned papers until the grading period is over.
- Assist your child with cleaning and organizing by starting the job together.
- Offer an incentive for meeting an organizational goal.
- Label your child's materials and possessions with his or her name.
- To avoid early-morning rush, have your child prepare for school the night before. Set out the next day's outfit, prepare lunch, load his or her backpack, shower or bathe.
- Have your child place his or her loaded backpack in the same spot every night.

See Checklist 4.6 for recommendations on how teachers can help their students with organization skills.

Time Management Strategies and Supports

Poor time management and awareness of how long it takes to complete tasks cause many problems for students in school and at home. Strengthen your child's time management skills by providing the necessary tools, modeling, teaching effective strategies, and providing your direct support.

Tools, Schedules, and Supports

- Help your child learn to tell time and read a nondigital (analog) clock as well as a calendar.
- Make sure that clocks in your home are accurate.
- Set electronic devices to ring or vibrate at certain times, to help your child remember appointments, observe curfews, or keep on schedule.
- Teach and model how to use to-do lists by writing down things to do, then crossing off accomplished tasks.
- Help your child schedule the evening and estimate how long each homework assignment or activity should take. Check the estimates afterwards to help improve future planning skills.
- Help your child develop the habit of using a personal planner, assignment calendar, assignment log, or agenda book. By the time children are in the middle to upper elementary grades, children should be recording assignments daily, using one of these tools.
- Your child may need assistance from a classmate, a buddy, or the teacher to be sure assignments are recorded. Discuss this task with the teacher. Ask your child to show you the calendar or planner every day after school.
- Post a large calendar or wall chart in a central location of the home for scheduling family activities and events. Encourage everyone to refer to it daily. Each family member may record on the calendar with his or her own specific colored pen.

- Help transfer important extracurricular activities and other scheduled events to your child's personal calendar or planner.

- Help your child create a weekly schedule.

- Have an older child take a few days to track and record how he or she spends time over the course of twenty-four hours. After a few days, your child should have better awareness of how much time is typically spent on routine activities: meals, sleeping, grooming, screen time (television, computer), talking on the phone, recreational and social activities, and study and homework time.

- Phone calls and electronic messages can interfere with staying on schedule and on task. Turn off cell phones and remove them from the room while children do homework. Checking messages and returning phone calls or text messages can be done during homework breaks. See Checklist 3.5.

Managing Routines

- Morning and evening routines for getting ready for school and preparing for bed are very helpful. Use clear reminders of the routine (for example, a checklist of sequential tasks to complete) to reduce nagging, rushing, and negative interactions.

- Checklists are tools for time management and staying on schedule. Have your child cross off each task when it is completed.

- Combine checklists and routines with a positive reinforcement system. For example, if all items are completed and checked off by a certain time, a small reward is earned.

- Help your child establish a routine for extracurricular activities. Include scheduled time for practice and gathering needed items (with the aid of a checklist).

Long-Term Projects

- Your assistance with time management and structuring of long-term school assignments, such as book reports and projects, is critical to your child's success. Build in plenty of time. When scheduling, allow for unforeseen glitches and delays.

- Help break down longer assignments into smaller, manageable chunks. Have your child mark deadlines on the calendar for completing each incremental step.

- Together with your child, record on a master calendar the due date of the final project and plan when to do the steps along the way (for example, going to the library for materials, taking notes).

- Pay close attention to due dates, and post project requirements.

- Ask teachers for feedback and help in monitoring whether your child is on track with a project. Do not assume that your child is working sufficiently on projects at school, even if he or she is given time in class to do so.

- Large projects can be overwhelming and discouraging. Provide assistance as needed and support in pacing and monitoring timelines toward project completion.

- See Checklist 3.5 for homework strategies including more ideas for supporting your child with long-term projects.

- See Checklists 4.2 and 4.6 for ideas on how teachers can support students' with time management and long-term homework projects.

3.8 Strategies for Building Your Child's Study Skills

There is no one study strategy that works best for all children. If students are exposed to a variety of reading and study strategies during their elementary, middle, and high school years, they begin to develop a repertoire of what is effective for them. Parents can help by introducing and reinforcing techniques, then evaluating their effectiveness together with their children when they study at home.

Use Multisensory Approaches

- Encourage your child to explain and teach you what he has learned. Also, provide opportunities for hands-on learning and immediate review. Research shows that many of us remember best what we actually practice by doing and material we teach to others.

- Incorporate multisensory ways of learning and studying. Each person has preferred modalities through which he or she learns best. Experiment with different methods to find a match for your child's learning style (or styles). Use study methods that tap into your child's preferred learning style.

  - *Visual methods*: using flash cards; looking at pictures, charts, or maps; visualizing; color coding.

  - *Auditory methods*: listening to someone read or explain; discussing; talking into a recorder, then listening to it; studying with music in the background; using songs, raps, chants, or rhymes to learn information.

  - *Tactile-kinesthetic methods*: writing down or typing information; tracing; drawing; graphing; demonstrating; acting it out; using manipulatives; studying while doing something physical (walking, jogging, using an exercise bike, bouncing a ball).

- Teach your child to use frequent review and practice in small amounts to learn large amounts of material.

- Have your child teach (or review) newly learned material to someone else.

- Suggest that your child create study cards by writing questions about the material to be studied on index cards and writing the answers on the back. These can be reviewed for a few minutes whenever the child has free moments in the day.

- To aid memory, have your child practice the technique of visualizing when reading. Read aloud to your child and stop periodically, asking for a description of what he or she sees in his or her mind's eye.

- See James Madison University Special Education Program's Learning Toolbox Web site (http://coe.jme.edu/Learning Toolbox) for learning strategies that are designed for students with learning disabilities in test taking and study skills. These strategies include some described in Checklists 2.7, 2.10, and 2.11 as well as this study skills strategy:

    CHECK

    Change environments (to one free from distractions).

    Have all equipment nearby.

    Establish rewards for yourself.

    Create a checklist of tasks to be done.

    Keep a "worry pad" (to write down distracting ideas that pop into your head).

- Use strategies found throughout this book (for example, graphic organizers) to help your child study.

Use Study Methods That Incorporate Active Learning

- **SQ3R:** This strategy increases comprehension and retention of textbook material, making it both a good reading and study strategy. It involves the following steps:

1. **Survey:** Briefly look over the reading assignment: titles, chapter headings, illustrations, charts, and graphs. Skim through the assignment and read the chapter summary and end-of-chapter questions.

2. **Question:** Turn the headings and subheadings of the text into questions. For example, *Producing Antibodies* can become "How do our bodies produce antibodies?" *Organic Motor Fuels* can become "What are the different organic motor fuels?"

3. **Read:** Read to find the answers to the questions developed in step 2. Identify the main ideas, and jot down any questions, notes, or unknown vocabulary.

4. **Recite:** At the end of each chapter section, state the gist of what was read. *Note:* Restating or summarizing into an audio recorder is often very effective.

5. **Review:** Check recall of important information from the reading. A study guide of some kind may be created. Reviewing over a number of days is very helpful.

- **SQ4R:** This strategy is the same as SQ3R, but with an additional step beginning with the /r/ sound—*Write*. The SQ4R procedure is survey, question, read, recite, write, and review. After a brief verbal summary of what the reading passage is about, students write the answers to the questions from step 2 and then review.

- **RCRC:** This study strategy involves these steps:
  1. **R**ead a portion of the material.
  2. **C**over that passage with hand or paper.
  3. **R**ecite, restating in your own words.
  4. **C**heck for accuracy by looking at the text again.

- **Note taking:** There are many note-taking techniques. Split note methods, such as the Cornell method, involve dividing a paper into columns and recording key information in those columns. Young children would use two columns with main ideas in words or pictures, or questions to be answered on the left side and details, definitions, or answers to the questions on the right side. When used with older students, this method involves the following steps:

1. Divide a paper into two columns.

2. The left column (about one-fourth to one-third of the width of the paper) is where key terms, questions, additions, and corrections are written. This column can be used while taking notes in class or later as a review of what was learned in class. The right column is about three-fourths or two-thirds of the width of the paper. This column is where the lecture notes are written in class (on the front side of the page only).

3. Students review their notes within twenty-four hours (preferably within three hours) after the lecture. During this time, they re-read and then fill in key terms and make additions or corrections in the left column.

4. Space is left at the bottom of the page for a summary.

Try Different Formats for Studying

Parents tend to think that their own children should work and study the way they once did. However, because children with dyslexia, like other children, have their own unique strengths and weaknesses, respecting what works for them becomes especially important. Encourage your child to try these ways to study:

- Study with a partner or study group.
- Try studying at different times of day (such as weekend mornings or after dinner) to find the times when focus is the best.
- Have a parent make up a sample test on the material.
- Verbalize the material. Talk it out with someone.

- Study in motion (listening to an audio recording while riding a stationary bike or jogging).
- Find a comfortable study chair or couch away from distractions.
- Break large amounts of material into smaller segments. For example, review notes for twenty minutes a day for ten days rather than for longer periods right before the test.
- Create a packet of study guides or graphic organizers that can be used to prepare for a test.
- Use board games as a way to study. For example, when you land on a marked space, pick a card with a multiplication fact or a geography term. After providing the correct answer, you get to move again.
- Play card games with separate question and answer cards. Match the question card with its correct answer.
- When a test is returned, look it over in order to figure out mistakes. Discuss with a friend or parent whether the way you studied worked. Why or why not?

Resources

Brooks, R., & Goldstein, S. (2001). *Raising resilient children: Fostering strength, hope, and optimism in your child.* Chicago: Contemporary Books.

Cohen, M. (2009). *A guide to special education advocacy: What parents, clinicians, and advocates need to know.* Philadelphia: Kingsley.

Currie, P. S., & Wadlington, E. M. (2000). *The source for learning disabilities.* East Moline, IL: LinguiSystems.

Frishman, S. R. *Special Education Advocacy 101.* (n.d.). Retrieved from the Internet Special Education Resources Web site at http://www.iser .com/resources/advocacy-terms.html

Greene, J. F., & Moats, L. C. (2000). *Testing: Critical components in the identification of dyslexia* (International Dyslexia Association Fact Sheet No. 976). Retrieved from http://www.dyslexia-test.com/ida.html

Howey, P. (2009). *10 tips for good advocates.* Retrieved from http://www .wrightslaw.com/howey/10tips.advocates.htm

LD Online. (1998). *Advocacy in action: You can advocate for your child!.* Retrieved from http://www.ldonline.org/article/5910

Moats, L. C., & Dakin, K. E. (2008). *Basic facts about dyslexia and other reading problems.* Baltimore: International Dyslexia Association.

National Center for Learning Disabilities. (2009). *IDEA terms to know.* Retrieved from National Center for Learning Disabilities Web site: http://www.ncld.org/resources1/glossaries/idea-terms-to-know

National Center for Learning Disabilities. (2009). *Self-esteem fact sheet.* Retrieved from National Center for Learning Disabilities Web site: http://www.ncld.org/ld-basics/ld-aamp-social-skills/self-esteem/ self-esteem-fact-sheet

Parents' Educational Resource Center. (1995). *Bridges to reading: Building self-esteem and dealing with disappointments at school.* San Mateo, CA: Parents' Educational Resource Center.

Rief, S. (2003). *The ADHD book of lists: A practical guide for helping children and teens with attention deficit disorders.* San Francisco: Jossey-Bass.

Rief, S. (2005). *How to reach and teach children with ADD/ADHD* (2nd ed.). San Francisco: Jossey-Bass.

Rief, S. (2008). *The ADD/ADHD checklist: A practical reference for parents and teachers* (2nd ed.). San Francisco: Jossey-Bass.

Schwed, A., & Melichar-Utter, J. (2008). *Brain-friendly study strategies.* Thousand Oaks, CA: Corwin Press.

Siegel, L. (2007). *Nolo's IEP guide: Learning disabilities.* Berkeley, CA: Nolo Press.

Silver, L. B. (2006). *The misunderstood child: Understanding and coping with your child's learning disabilities* (4th ed.). New York: Three Rivers Press.

Sirotowitz, S., Davis, L., & Parker, H. C. (2003). *Study strategies for early school success.* Plantation, FL: Specialty Press.

Stern, J., & Quinn, P. (2008). *Putting on the brakes: Understanding and taking control of your ADD or ADHD* (2nd ed.). Washington, DC: Magination Press.

Stern, J., & Quinn, P. (2009). *Putting on the brakes: Activity book for kids with ADD or ADHD* (2nd ed.). Washington, DC: Magination Press.

Townend, J., & Turner, M. (2000). *Dyslexia in practice: A guide for teachers.* New York: Kluwer Academic/Plenum.

Wright, P., & Wright, P. (2006). *Wrightslaw: From emotions to advocacy—The special education survival guide* (2nd ed.). Hartfield, VA: Harbor House Law Press.

4

CHECKLISTS FOR TEACHERS

Introduction

4.1. Adaptations, Accommodations, and Modifications: What's the Difference?

4.2. How Teachers Can Help Students with Homework

4.3. Differentiating Instruction

4.4. Adaptations and Modifications of Materials

4.5. Adaptations and Accommodations in Testing

4.6. Helping Students with Organization and Time Management

4.7. Strategies to Aid Memory

4.8. Strategies for Teaching Reading in the Content Areas

Resources

Introduction

Teaching students with dyslexia has its challenges and rewards. Students with reading difficulties require accommodations, extra attention, and a repertoire of effective strategies from their teachers. Perhaps equally important are a teacher's willingness to try new things, to be flexible, and to view students as capable and intelligent people who also have learning problems. Students with dyslexia have the same capacity for becoming excited about learning as do their peers. Good teachers find ways to make this happen.

4.1 Adaptations, Accommodations, and Modifications: What's the Difference?

The difference between the terms *adaptations, accommodations*, and *modifications* can be confusing. First, let's clarify the meanings.

Adaptations

Adaptations are any adjustments in the curriculum, instructional components, environmental elements, or requirements or expectations of the student. Adaptations are part of what teachers do to meet the needs of diverse learners. A good teacher attempts to differentiate instruction and make adjustments to enable all students to succeed. The purpose of adaptations is to increase a student's academic achievement and social, emotional, and behavioral functioning. Adaptations in the general education curriculum, intended in federal laws to protect the rights of students with disabilities (IDEA and Section 504), are changes permissible to allow the student equal opportunity to access, results, and benefits in the least restrictive setting. Adaptations may involve adjustments or changes in the following areas:

- Materials
- Methods
- Teaching strategies
- Pacing
- Environment
- Assignments
- Task demands
- Grading
- Testing or evaluation
- Feedback
- Lesson presentation

- Reinforcement
- Student demonstration of understanding or mastery of content
- Student response opportunities
- Location
- Scheduling
- Level of support
- Degree of participation
- Time allotted
- Size or quantity of task or assignment

Adaptations include accommodations and modifications.

Accommodations

Accommodations are adaptations that do not fundamentally change the performance standards, instructional level, or content of what the student is expected to learn. The curricular content and expectations for performance and mastery are the same as for other students in the class or grade. Accommodations are provisions that enable a student to

- Better access the general education curriculum
- Learn and demonstrate mastery of content
- Meet the same performance goals that other students in the classroom or grade level are expected to achieve

Accommodations typically include adaptations or adjustments such as

- Extended time to complete tasks or tests
- Change of location (for testing)
- Extra support or assistance (peer, buddy, cross-age tutor, more small-group instruction)

- Assistance with organization or time management (keeping track of materials, recording assignments, breaking down large assignments)
- Providing tools or aids to support learning (outlines, graphic organizers, study guides, assistive technology, audio books)
- Note-taking assistance
- Computer access
- Preferential seating to enable a student to focus better during class and to receive more direct and frequent prompting, monitoring, and feedback from the teacher
- Reduction in the length of an assignment
- Allowing a student to dictate answers to a scribe
- Allowing a student to take a large test by doing one page at a time
- An oral reader for some tests
- Allowing a student to take a test by giving answers orally
- Providing a student with a written set of directions as a backup to orally presented information

Modifications

Modifications are adaptations that do alter or change in some way what the student is learning (the content or part of the curriculum). They also change to some degree the performance standards—the expectations for that student compared with what is required of his or her peers in the same classroom or grade.

Examples of modifications include

- Giving a student a different or alternative assignment. For example, a student may be assigned to write a single paragraph on a topic and draw an illustration rather than write a five-paragraph essay.

- Working with instructional materials at a lower level than other students of that grade.

- Using a reading anthology from a lower grade level rather than a grade-level text when the class is doing a unit on comparing short stories.

- Providing some students with a partially filled-in graphic organizer for a science lab experiment rather than the blank one used by their classmates.

- Reducing the number of words that a child needs to learn for a spelling test or testing him or her on different words.

- Providing an alternative form of a test to a student.

- Using a different report card format. For example, a student may receive a narrative report card rather than grades, or he or she may be graded according to different standards from those used to measure the majority of students.

- Allowing students in middle school or high school to have a modified class schedule. For example, they might be given an extra study hall or not be required to take a foreign language.

Using Adaptations to Help Students with Dyslexia

For students with disabilities, necessary accommodations and modifications are educational rights, not favors granted by teachers or school staff. It is generally recommended that accommodations be tried whenever possible before more significant modifications in curriculum or work expectations are made. However, students with dyslexia typically require both accommodations and modifications. They need to build reading competency through instruction and materials at an appropriate level in order to strengthen and practice skills. They often need compensatory methods, tools, and supports to enable them to access grade-level curriculum.

4.2 How Teachers Can Help
Students with Homework

Teachers can use many methods to support and build a good relationship between the home and school of a child with dyslexia. It typically takes students with learning disabilities more time to do homework than the average student, even with parental supervision and direct assistance. Assignments that may take their classmates twenty minutes to complete can easily be an hour of work for students with dyslexia. Adjustments that a teacher can make to help students with learning disabilities succeed include these:

- Be responsive to parents of students with disabilities who report great frustration in regard to homework. Be willing to make adjustments so that these students spend a reasonable amount of time doing their homework. Shorten assignments or reduce the amount of writing required.

- Many teachers have a practice of sending home unfinished class work. Avoid this if possible. While some class assignments need to be completed at home, try to find alternatives for students with learning disabilities. Provide the necessary modifications and supports so that class work gets done during school, not as extra homework.

- Remember that homework should be a time for reviewing and practicing what students have been taught in class. Assignments should not involve new information that parents are expected to teach to their children.

- Homework should not be busywork. Make homework relevant and purposeful so that time spent is helpful in reinforcing skills or concepts that were taught.

- Do not add on homework as a punishment or negative consequence for misbehavior at school.

- Avoid unnecessary copying and recopying or high standards of neatness for students with dyslexia.

- Visually post homework assignments in addition to explaining them. Write assignments in a consistent location of the classroom (on a corner of the board or on a chart stand, for example).

- Modify homework for students with disabilities. Reducing the written output required is particularly helpful. Ask yourself these questions: What is the goal? What do I want students to learn from the assignment? Can they get the concepts without having to do all the writing? Can they practice the skills in an easier, more motivating format? Can they practice the skills by doing fewer problems?

- If you have extra copies of textbooks to lend to parents, do so for students who are forgetful and frequently leave the books they need at home or school.

- If writing is difficult for a student, encourage him or her to do assignments on a computer or give permission for specific assignments to be dictated to a parent or tutor.

Communicate Clearly

- Read homework instructions aloud. Make sure you have explained the assignments carefully and clarified students' questions.

- If your school has modernized communication between home and school by providing homework hot lines, teacher Web pages or other class Web sites, or voicemail, use them regularly. Keep information for parents and students up-to-date.

- Consider assigning homework, when possible, at the beginning of the period rather than at the end. Make sure it is written down so that students can see it as well as hear it.

- Provide students with written reminders of assignments that are missing, so that they have an opportunity to catch up before parents need to be notified.

- Communicate regularly with parents of students who are falling behind in homework. Do not wait until the student is so far behind in completing work that catching up becomes impossible. For example, use a monitoring form that indicates missing assignments or notify parents by phone or e-mail at specific intervals about missing or incomplete assignments.

- When assigning a long-term project or report, consider calling the parents of some students. Even if you have discussed the assignment in class and provided written information, parents may not know about it. Ask parents to check their child's notebook for the written information about the project, or volunteer to send another copy to post at home. A "heads up" to parents about the assignment will be appreciated.

- Communicate with other teachers on your team. Students who have several teachers are often assigned a number of tests, large projects, and reading assignments all at the same time. Be sensitive to scheduling. Stagger due dates and coordinate whenever possible with other teachers to avoid the heavy stress of everything being due at the same time.

- Ask parents to let you know if their child is spending too much time on homework or expressing significant frustration or lack of understanding. Agree on time limits so that a child has needed free time every evening.

Provide Monitoring and Support

- Supervise students who tend to be forgetful before they leave at the end of the day. Make sure that they have their materials, books, and assignments recorded and in their backpack.

- Assign a study buddy to your students with learning disabilities. Study buddies are responsible, willing classmates whom they can phone or e-mail in the evening to ask questions about homework or to find out what they missed on days when they were absent.

- An important way to help students (and their parents) keep on top of homework, tests, and long-term projects is to require students to use an assignment sheet, calendar, or planner. Then guide and monitor the recording of assignments. Make this a daily expectation and routine, so everyone will benefit.

- Check and initial students' assignment calendar, sheet, or planner every day, if needed.

- Have parents initial the assignment planner, calendar, or sheet daily. Designate a place for parents and teacher to write notes to each other—an excellent system for communication between home and school.

- Work with your school on the possibility of providing supervised study halls, homework labs or clubs, tutorials, or other assistance for students who need it.

- Collect homework, and provide feedback when you return it. It is frustrating to students and parents to spend a lot of time on assignments that are not collected.

- Allow students to e-mail homework to you, to avoid lost assignments.

- For long-term projects or large tests, provide students with a written timeline or checklist of intermediate deadlines to encourage appropriate pacing of the work.

- Make yourself available at a specified time at least once or twice a week (before school, during lunch) so that students can come to you to ask homework questions or get feedback on work they have started.

Keep Things in Perspective

- Students with disabilities benefit from participation in extra-curricular activities. They need opportunities to develop areas of strength and interest (for example, athletics, dance, art, and music) that can be sources of good self-esteem and motivation. These nonacademic after-school activities are important for students' development. Be flexible and willing to make adjustments in the homework load to accommodate extracurricular activities, differentiating homework assignments as needed.

- Many students with dyslexia work with tutors or counselors and participate in programs outside of school to boost skills and receive intervention services. Consider those factors when assigning homework.

- Remind parents that you do not expect to see perfectly done homework with no errors. Homework is a tool for seeing what students can do independently. It is not the parent's job to make sure that everything is correct.

Find Ways to Increase Motivation

- Try to make assignments interesting. Build in student options. For example, tell students to select three of the five questions to answer or choose one of three topics offered.

- Include homework that incorporates an element of play or fun, such as a learning game to reinforce or practice a skill.

- Write goals for improvement in homework performance together with the student (and a parent if possible). If, for example, the child turns in less than 50 percent of homework assignments during a typical week, the initial goal might be to turn in 60 or 70 percent of weekly assignments, gradually raising the goal to 80 percent and then 90 percent as the student achieves success.

- Reward students for completing and turning in homework with extra points, tangible treats, "one free homework" passes, "one late homework without penalty" passes, special privileges, or other positive reinforcements.

- See the Web site www.homeworkopoly.com for a tool and a method to motivate students to turn in their homework.
- See Checklists 2.15, 4.3, and 4.6 for more information about work assigned, and Checklists 3.5 and 3.8 for recommendations to parents on this topic.

Additional Homework Adaptations and Accommodations

- Allow students to create products other than written ones (for example, let students make a poster, write a song, or prepare a PowerPoint presentation) in order to show understanding of a concept.
- Allow students to turn in an audio recording of answers to questions instead of written responses.
- Accept homework that is dictated by a student to a parent scribe.
- Let students begin homework at school with support.
- Be flexible on giving credit for work that is turned in late.
- Allow students to turn in long-term assignments in parts, as they are completed.
- Provide a specific place in the classroom where students turn in homework, as well as a place where they can find copies of assignments they missed or need to redo.
- Give students a separate grade for content, so that mechanical errors in writing do not negate good ideas and effort.
- Hold discussions in class about common homework problems and how to solve them (for example, discuss balancing after-school activities with homework, what to do when a child is unsure of how to do an assignment, or forgets a book at school).

4.3 Differentiating Instruction

Differentiated instruction is a way of thinking about teaching and learning that recognizes the fact that one size does not fit all learners. This is certainly true for students with dyslexia and other learning disabilities. Teachers can use numerous ways to differentiate instruction, including

- Multiple and flexible groupings of students
- Multisensory instruction
- Varying degrees of support
- Choices of where, how, and with whom students may work
- Choices about topics of study, ways of learning, modes of expression
- Assignments, projects, and student products that draw on students' individual strengths and interests
- Accommodations and modifications for individual students
- Varied approaches to lesson presentation, assignments, materials, and assessment that take into account learning styles, individual interests, and talents

Lesson Presentation

- Address students' learning style differences and preferences, providing auditory, visual, and tactile or kinesthetic input.
- Use high-interest materials.
- Write key words and illustrate throughout your presentation, even if you lack the skill or talent to draw well.
- Use technology in instruction when possible (document cameras, interactive whiteboards, video streaming, PowerPoint presentations)

- Incorporate demonstrations, role playing, hands-on activities, anecdotes and storytelling, and multimedia presentations into your teaching.
- Build in opportunities for movement during the lesson.
- Increase the novelty of tasks by using a game format or providing different materials for students to use, such as dry-erase boards and colored markers rather than paper and pencils.
- Give multisensory instructions (not just oral or written ones).
- Ensure that students understood your directions; see if they are able to restate them.
- Use visuals, charts, and models for student reference.
- Increase the amount of practice and review.
- Use concrete manipulatives and hands-on approaches to enhance learning.
- Use technology and games for skill practice.
- Provide opportunities to preview new material before it is taught in class, such as seeing an outline of an upcoming lesson.
- Consult with a special education teacher or other staff member for how to teach concepts or skills in different ways.
- Consider a variety of ways to provide students access to your lectures or class review sessions either as an additional opportunity to listen again and supplement what they heard in class, or to enable absent students to hear what they missed. For example,
  - Allow students to bring their own recording device to class.
  - Record and upload to a Web site (your own or school's) the lecture after it has been presented in class.
  - Keep recorded lectures on a flash drive, memory stick, CD, or any file-holding device to provide to students when needed.

- Allow students to download your recording onto their personal MP3 player devices, such as an IPod.

Questioning

- Increase opportunities for active student involvement in the lesson; use these techniques for inclusive and engaging questioning:
    - Ask open-ended questions to stimulate critical thinking and discussion.
    - Before asking for a verbal response to a question, have students jot down their best guess. Call for volunteers to answer.
    - Provide at least five seconds of waiting time when asking a student to respond.
    - Pose a question, ask for volunteers, and wait until several hands are raised before calling on individuals to respond.
- Partner activities are an excellent format for keeping students engaged and productive and are a safe way for students to respond to questions in that they cause less anxiety. Pair students with dyslexia with a cooperative, supportive classmate. Use some of these partner activities:
    - "Pair up with your neighbor, and share your ideas about . . . "
    - "Turn to your partner and summarize (or paraphrase) your understanding of . . ." After giving partners a chance to respond, ask for volunteers to share with the class: "Who would like to share what you and your partner thought about . . . ?"
    - "Write down with your partner all the things you can think of that . . ."
    - "Help each other figure out how to . . ."

- "With your partner, clarify questions you still have about what we just discussed."

Assignments

- Provide options for demonstrating mastery of concepts or skills through alternatives to writing (oral exams, projects, demonstrations, visual displays).
- Offer choices in assignments (various topics and levels of difficulty, options for working independently or with a partner or small group).
- Offer project or assignment options that draw on a range of strengths and interests.
- Provide sentence starters, topic sentences, or frames as scaffolds for students who have difficulty with starting writing assignments.
- Provide direct, guided instruction before students work on an assignment independently.
- Monitor closely as students begin an assignment, to ensure that they understand the task. Provide assistance, if needed.
- Allow different ways of getting an assignment done. For example, allow a student to type or dictate to a scribe or record work on a digital recorder instead of writing.
- Structure assignments so that they are broken down into smaller segments. Assign one part at a time.
- Check assignments midway through (or sooner) so that you can give corrective feedback.
- If a page of work is overwhelming, provide it in parts. For example, cut up the page and pass out one row of problems at a time.
- Provide a rubric that describes expectations for assignments, including specific evaluation criteria.

- Provide written task cards or checklists of things to do when assigning seatwork.
- Be sure that students are actually capable of doing assignments for independent work on their own, or provide peer or adult assistance.
- Reduce paper-and-pencil tasks.
- Shorten assignments.
- Allow students to use cursive handwriting or printing (whichever is easier and more legible).
- Reduce the amount of required copying from the board or books. Instead, provide a photocopy or copying assistance.
- Provide computer access for students who wish to use it for their written work.
- Provide audio recordings of texts.
- Provide extended time for completion of assignments.
- Adjust the reading level of the assignment.
- Modify homework as needed, and be responsive to parent feedback.

4.4 Adaptations and Modifications of Materials

- Provide an array of learning materials and books that span the range of reading levels of your students in order to differentiate instruction. For example, if the class is studying inventors, provide an assortment of resources on inventors that range from easy reading through more challenging levels.

- Adapt and have available textbooks that are highlighted in different colors for key information and key words (main ideas and important vocabulary).

- Provide students with tactile materials like finger paints or colored sand trays for writing, so that the various textures reinforce learning through touch.

- Set up creative learning centers with hands-on materials for students to work with independently, with partners, or in small groups.

- Provide access to audio books and recordings of textbooks.

- Provide consumable copies of tests so that students can write directly on the page or test booklet instead of having to copy answers onto another page or answer sheet.

- Provide photocopied pages instead of requiring students to copy from the board or a book onto paper.

- Experiment with different kinds of graph paper and lined paper. Some children with writing difficulties can write more neatly within smaller or narrower lines; others do better with wider lines.

- If fine motor control is a problem, have students experiment with pencil grips to find one that is comfortable.

- Provide markers (strips of cardboard or window box frames) for students who lose their place when reading.

- Provide computer access and other assistive technology. For more on this topic, see Checklists 2.13 and 2.14.

- Structure materials to enhance attention:
  - Block the page or fold it so that only part of the material is shown at one time.
  - Frame the material.
  - Highlight, underline, circle, or draw arrows and boxes in vivid colors.
  - Provide clear, clean copies of handouts that are well organized and easy to read.
  - Use illustrations and graphics.
  - Enlarge type size and spacing on the page
  - Rearrange the page format to simplify and reduce visual distractions.
- Use materials that increase the rate and immediacy of feedback:
  - Flash cards with answers on the back for immediate checking and correction
  - Computer programs for practicing basic skills: spelling, word recognition, math facts, vocabulary
  - Interactive educational software and online programs for teaching and reinforcing academic skills

  Note: Elements of self-correction, self-pacing, and competition against oneself or a computer (not another peer) are less threatening for children with learning difficulties and low self-esteem.

- Consider using a digital recorder in these ways:
  - Record directions and specific instructions for tasks, so that students can listen as many times as necessary.
  - Record text chapters and literature that students can listen to, preferably while following along with the text.
  - Record test questions for students to respond to verbally or in writing.

- Record lectures, assignments, and class reviews prior to exams as described in Checklist 4.3.

- Allow students to use a personal recorder for self-reminders, such as recording the homework assignment at the end of the class period.

- Recommend that students use a recorder as a study tool for verbalizing information and rehearsing before performance tasks.

- Use math material supports and adaptations:

  - Reduce the number of problems on a page.

  - Use frames, boxes, or windows to separate and space problems.

  - Use graph paper to structure the placement of numerals and help with the alignment and organization of problems.

  - Use an assortment of colorful manipulatives (pattern blocks, tiles, cubes, number lines, dice) to teach and reinforce number concepts (quantity, fractions, geometry, patterning).

  - Have students use calculators to solve problems and to check work after paper-and-pencil calculations.

  - Provide students with reference tools (charts of multiplication tables or formulas, lists of measurements and conversions).

  - Provide a card file or notebook for students to insert cards or pages showing steps, procedures, and examples of various math problems and algorithms taught in class.

4.5 Adaptations and Accommodations in Testing

This checklist contains a list of adaptations to support students in developing test-taking skills and to consider in designing exams that will be a fair assessment of all students' learning. Also included in this checklist are testing accommodations and modifications for students with dyslexia who may be unable to demonstrate their comprehension or mastery of the content material under normal testing conditions and criteria.

To help all students perform their best on tests,

- Provide tests that are easy to read: typed, written in clear language, at least double-spaced, cleanly printed, with ample margins. Avoid handwritten tests.
- Prior to testing, conduct extensive reviews with students.
- Eliminate unnecessary words and confusing language on tests.
- State directions in clear terms and simple sentences.
- Underline directions or key words in directions, set them in boldface type, or highlight them with color.
- Provide opportunities for short-answer assessments. For example, use multiple-choice, matching, or fill-in-the-blank items.
- On vocabulary tests, give the definition and have the student supply the word instead of providing the word and requiring the student to write out the definition.
- For fill-in-the-blank tests, provide a word bank from which students can select the correct word for the blanks.
- Provide students ahead of time with examples of different types of test questions that will be on the exam.
- Administer frequent short quizzes throughout the teaching unit and review them the next day, thus providing feedback to students on their understanding of the material.

- Read directions aloud for each section of the test before students begin the exam.

- Teach students strategies and skills for taking a variety of tests: true-false, multiple-choice, fill-in-the-blank, essay. Practice different formats and discuss strategies for each.

- Give students the opportunity to write their own test questions in different formats.

- Test only what has been taught.

- Provide generous writing space, especially for math problems and essay questions.

- Avoid questions that are worded to deliberately trick students.

- After reading the directions aloud to the class, read them again to students who need additional clarification.

- Write multiple-choice questions with choices listed vertically rather than horizontally; this format is easier to read.

- Use portfolio assessment, in which progress is evaluated on individual performance and improvement rather than comparison with other students.

- For a change of routine, occasionally assign take-home tests.

- Reduce the weight of a single test grade. Consider having several shorter, more frequent quizzes rather than lengthy unit tests.

- Allow students to use graph paper or other paper to solve math problems and attach the paper to the test rather than requiring that computation be done in the limited work space directly on the test.

- Divide a test into parts, administering each part on different days rather than rushing students to complete lengthy tests in one class period.

- Do not penalize students for spelling, grammar, or other mechanics on tests that measure mastery of content in other areas.
- Permit the use of earplugs or other devices in order to block out auditory distractions.
- Provide privacy boards for students' desks, to reduce visual distractions during test taking.

Test-Taking Accommodations and Modifications

- Administer the test in a different location, such as a resource room, individually, or in a small group.
- Read the test questions to the student.
- Administer the exam in the classroom, then in a small group or individually (supervised by a special education teacher or other adult). Average the two grades.
- Allow students with writing disabilities to retake tests orally after taking them in writing, in order to add points if they are able to demonstrate greater mastery than they were able to show on the written test. This technique is especially helpful in the case of essay questions.
- Substitute an oral test for a written test, or allow the student to answer questions orally, elaborating on what he or she wrote to provide a more accurate assessment of his or her learning.
- Permit students to record answers to essay questions on an audio recorder rather than write them or in addition to writing responses.
- Provide audio-recorded test questions so that students can go back and listen to questions as many times as needed.
- Before assigning the final grade on a test, point out some test items that you spot as incorrect and allow students to self-correct careless errors before scoring.

- Give reduced spelling lists for students with spelling disabilities—for example, ten words rather than twenty. When dictating words for the test, dictate those ten words first; then continue with the other words for the rest of the class. Students who are tested on reduced spelling lists have the option of trying the additional words for bonus points.

- Score tests based on the number of correct items out of the total number assigned for a specific student. (The total number assigned can be shortened for individual students.)

- Eliminate the need for students to copy test questions from the board or a book before answering. Allow students to write directly in the test booklet.

- Seat students near the teacher or in an optimal location for teacher monitoring and focusing, if they need it.

- Permit an adult to serve as a scribe and record the student's answers.

- Administer the test at a different time of the day or in shorter intervals over several different sessions.

- Provide extended time for testing.

- Allow a calculator and a multiplication table on tests that assess problem-solving skills, not computation.

- Revise test formats as needed (reduced number of items on a page, increased spacing between items, simplified vocabulary, larger font size). Ask special educators for advice.

- Permit brief breaks during testing.

Accommodations for Standardized Testing

In addition to taking classroom tests, most students will take some form of high-stakes test during their school years. State and district school systems may use these types of tests during the elementary through high school years as a form of group assessment. Private schools make use of standardized group tests to monitor student and school progress. College entrance exams are taken by many students as part of the college application process. With appropriate documentation, students with dyslexia may be entitled to accommodations in high-stakes test settings so that they can demonstrate what they know without the barriers caused by their disabilities.

An example of some testing accommodations that can be made available to students, depending on the nature and severity of their disabilities, as well as the specific tests given and the adequacy of the documentation, include

- Extended time
- Large-print test booklets
- Human reader (reads test or directions orally to student)
- Computer use
- Reduced number of test items on each page
- Use of scribe to write student's answers
- Audio recorder, so that answers can be spoken
- Permission to write answers directly in test booklet
- Testing in another room or at another test site
- Testing in an individual or small-group setting
- Preferential seating
- Breaks between tests

Under IDEA and Section 504, students with disabilities need to be considered for testing accommodations by submitting documentation for review and following specific procedures to determine eligibility. Parents should work together with school personnel or private evaluators to apply for appropriate test accommodations if they are needed.

For more information about standardized testing accommodations for college-bound high school students with disabilities, visit the following Web sites:

- http://www.act.org/aap/disab/
- http://professionals.collegeboard.com/ testing/ssd/accommodations

4.6 Helping Students with Organization and Time Management

Some of the greatest difficulties that many students experience involve poor organization and time-management skills—particularly for those with learning disabilities or executive functioning weaknesses. There are many ways teachers can help students develop these important life skills.

Organization

It is important to teach all students organizational skills. For those with dyslexia, various supports and accommodations are often necessary for them to achieve school success.

Help Students Organize Supplies and Materials

- Require the use of a three-ring binder or notebook starting in third grade. An accordion folder for maintaining papers by subject may work for students who cannot work with a binder.
- Have students use colored subject dividers in their notebook, as well as a pencil pouch in which they can keep a few sharpened pencils with erasers and other small supplies.
- Younger students (kindergarten through second grade) can use a pocket folder for carrying papers to and from school.
- Require students to carry a backpack or book bag and bring their notebook, binder, or homework folder to and from school.
- Teach students how to keep papers organized by placing them in the appropriate subject section of their binder.
- Require the use of a monthly assignment calendar or planner or a daily or weekly assignment sheet that is kept at the front of the student's binder. Calendars, student planners, or assignment sheets and student handouts should all be three-hole-punched for storage in the binder. Have students

consistently record all classroom assignments. Model and monitor the process.

- Suggest a consistent location in the binder for storing home-work assignments (or work to do and work to turn in)—for example,

  - Colored, hole-punched pocket folders can be inserted into the binder. One folder can be labeled *Homework*, while a different colored folder may be for graded and returned papers or papers to leave at home.

  - Large laminated envelopes that are three-hole-punched can be inserted into the binder in order to store home-work and assorted project papers.

- Encourage students to keep a supply of notebook paper in a consistent location in their binder.

- Keep spare supplies on hand so that time isn't wasted by stu-dents' searching or asking around to borrow from classmates.

- Encourage students to organize materials upon arriving in class and before dismissal.

- Provide adhesive hole reinforcers for ripped-out papers and plastic sleeves for papers that students don't want to punch holes in.

- Encourage students to keep their daily reference tools (for example, a multiplication chart or list of frequently misspelled words) in a specific section of their notebook or binder.

- Designate specific places in the room (trays, color-coded folders, or boxes) for students to turn in assignments or store unfinished work.

Use Color to Organize
- Color coordinate by subject area, to make locating materials quicker and easier. For example, have students cover the science text in yellow paper or put a yellow adhesive dot

on the binding; use a yellow notebook, lab book, or folder for science; and highlight the science class period and room number in yellow. The divider for science in the binder would also be yellow.

- Prepare important notices and handouts on colored paper, preferably color-coded—for example, newsletters in blue, spelling lists in pink.
- Use brightly colored paper for project assignments, providing details and due dates. Provide two copies (one for the binder and one to be posted at home).

Monitor, Support, and Motivate

- Have periodic desk and binder checks.
- Positively reinforce good organizational habits with prizes, certificates, or "no homework tonight" coupons for passing binder or work space inspections.
- Provide bonus points for improved organization. Reward your typically disorganized students when they are able to quickly locate a certain book or paper in their desk or binder.
- Provide time and assistance for cleaning out desks and binders and sorting papers.
- At the end of the day, make sure that students have necessary books or materials in their backpack to take home.
- Provide peer or adult assistance to help disorganized students organize desks, backpacks, and binders. Have them refile papers in the appropriate section of their binder and throw away trash.

Try These Organizational Tips

- Provide models for how to organize papers (for example, a sample paper with proper headings, margins, and spacing).
- Provide models of well-organized projects.

- Allow natural consequences for not having materials. Do not positively reinforce students who are unprepared by giving or loaning them new, desirable materials or supplies. Only let students borrow from a supply of less desirable materials. Keep a box of golf pencils or old pencils and erasers for this purpose.

Time Awareness and Time Management

Students with dyslexia often underestimate how much time they will need to complete a task. They may have difficulty in meeting deadlines and due dates and may require assistance from teachers or parents or need accommodations at school in order to complete their work in a timely fashion.

Assignment Sheets, Calendars, and Student Planners

- Communicate and maintain a clear expectation that all assignments will be recorded on students' assignment calendar or planner.
- Model the recording of homework assignments in the student planner, calendar, or assignment sheet, using a transparency or with a document camera. At the beginning or end of the period, lead students in recording assignments on their calendars or planners.
- Check and initial the assignment sheet, calendar, or planner.
- Supervise students as they leave at the end of class. Make sure that they have materials, books, and recorded assignments in their backpacks.
- Routinely ask table partners or groups seated together to check each other so that assignments are accurately recorded.
- Assign study buddies so that students can help each other. These partners can be responsible for checking each other to make sure that assignments are recorded on their calendar or

planner. When a student is absent, the buddy can collect all handouts, notices, and assignments for the absent student.

- Keep a master copy of the assignment calendar or student planner up-to-date and accessible for students to copy. This practice is especially important for students who are pulled out of the classroom during the day or who are absent.

- Provide students with a single- or double-page monthly calendar on which to record due dates of projects, tests, and important activities or events.

- Maintain a posted calendar in class and refer to it.

- Visually post homework assignments in addition to explaining them. Write the assignments in a consistent location in the classroom (on a corner of the board or a chart on a stand).

- For students who need extra monitoring, require that their parents initial their assignment calendar daily. This practice also provides a good way to communicate with parents.

Schedules

- Establish a daily routine and schedule for the classroom.

- Post schedules and refer to them throughout the day.

- Discuss the schedule each day and point out any changes in routine.

- With younger students, use a pictorial schedule that depicts the daily routine.

- For students who are receiving special education or related services, write down their weekly schedules and tape them to their desks or attach them to the cover of their notebooks.

- Encourage students and parents to plan a weekly schedule, including an established study and homework schedule. Encourage parents to help their children become aware of the time spent in a typical day on all activities from school dismissal until bedtime.

Long-Term Projects

- Structure long-term assignments (book reports, research projects) by breaking them into manageable increments.

- Make sure that students have access to needed materials.

- Assign incremental due dates to help structure a timeline for project completion. Establish due dates for stages of the project (getting a topic approved, submitting an outline, listing notes or resources, turning in a first draft).

- Call attention to due dates. Post due dates and frequently refer to them as reminders.

- Call some parents to make sure they are aware of the project and have at least one copy of the handout that explains guidelines for the project.

- Suggest to parents that they monitor timelines and help with pacing (for example, promptly get their child started on gathering resources).

- Monitor progress by asking to see what the student has accomplished, and provide feedback along the way.

Other Ways to Help with Time Management

- Provide students with a course outline or syllabus.

- Assist with prioritization of activities and workload.

- Teach students how to tell time and read a nondigital clock.

- Teach students how to read calendars and schedules.

- Make sure that all assignments, page numbers, and due dates are presented to students both orally and visually.

- Use to-do lists, modeling for the class how to write down and cross off accomplished tasks.

- Attach a list of specific things to do to students' desks, and monitor the practice of crossing off accomplished items.

- Provide enough time during transitions to put material away and get organized for the next activity.

- Encourage older students to use their electronic devices that have things-to-do features.
- Set timers for transitions. ("You have five minutes to finish working and put away your materials.")
- Teach students how to self-monitor on-task behavior so that they use class time effectively.
- If tardiness is an issue, try an individual contract with an incentive for being on time.
- Provide extended time as needed; consider flexibility regarding late work.
- Use frequent praise and positive reinforcement. Reward students for meeting deadlines and finishing assignments on time.

4.7 Strategies to Aid Memory

Difficulties with memory and retention of information are common for individuals with dyslexia. Checklist 1.5 discusses short-term, working memory, and retrieval difficulties that are weaknesses associated with dyslexia and other learning disabilities.

Use Mnemonics

Mnemonics are memory devices that help people remember something by associating what they are trying to remember with something they already know. Mnemonics include techniques such as acronyms, acrostics, and keywords.

- Teach children to create first-letter mnemonics (acronyms and acrostics) to help them remember steps in a process or procedure, sequences, or other information.

Examples of Acronyms

- HOMES (the Great Lakes): Huron, Ontario, Michigan, Erie, and Superior.
- Roy G. Biv (the seven colors of the rainbow): red, orange, yellow, green, blue, indigo, violet.
- Some words we use are actually acronyms—for example, *scuba:* self-contained underwater breathing apparatus.

Examples of Acrostics

- Dead Monsters Smell Badly (the steps for long division: divide, multiply, subtract, bring down)
- Every Good Boy Does Fine (the sequence of lines in the treble clef): E, G, B, D, F.

- Please Excuse My Dear Aunt Sally (the order for solving algebraic equations): parentheses, exponents, multiplication, division, addition, subtraction.

- When students are learning new vocabulary words and their meanings, suggest that they try the keyword technique: Pair the new word with a similar-sounding familiar word that can be visualized. For example, to learn the word *felons*, which sounds like *melons* and means "criminals," visualize some melons in prison clothing marching to jail. See New Monic Books' Web site at www.vocabularycartoons.com for books that teach vocabulary words (including those needed to prepare for standardized tests) by using this technique of linking word associations that rhyme and visual associations in the form of humorous cartoons.

- To help students remember numbers (math facts or phone numbers, for instance), have them try this mnemonic device: Associate each number from 0 to 9 with a rhyming word that that can be visualized concretely (for example, two/shoe, three/tree, four/door, six/sticks), and then make an association for the numbers you are trying to memorize. For example, to learn $6 \times 4 = 24$ or $4 \times 6 = 24$, one can visualize a door (4) with a pile of sticks (6) in front of it, and think: "Every day (24 hours), someone leaves a pile of sticks in front of my door." See the programs Memory Joggers (www.memoryjoggers.com) and Times Tables the Fun Way (www.citycreek.com), which teach math facts using these techniques.

- Have students use mnemonics to help them spell the tricky parts of words. For example, to remember the *br* in Fe*br*uary, a student might think, "February is a cold month. . . . brrrr."

- Suggest that state or national capitals can be learned using mnemonics. For example, to remember that Springfield is the capital of Illinois, a student might think, "I can't spring out of bed when I'm ill." To remember that Amsterdam is the capital of the Netherlands, a student might think of hamsters running around in Never Never Land.

Use Music and Rhyme

- Raps, rhymes, and songs help in learning multiplication tables and other information (for example, U.S. presidents or steps in a cycle or process). Resources that teach through this method can be found on these Web sites:
  - www.songsforteaching.com
  - www.musicallyaligned.com
  - www.mathsongs.com
  - www.school-house-rock.com
- Create your own verses of information to learn and memorize, using familiar melodies like "Row, Row, Row Your Boat," "Frère Jacques," or "Twinkle, Twinkle, Little Star." This method facilitates memorization and makes learning more fun. Many people learned the sequence of the alphabet and the months of the year using this technique.
- Use rhymes to help students remember rules (for example, *i* before *e* except after *c*).

Try These Other Memory Tips

- Memory is strengthened by creating meaningful links and associations. Look for ways that items go together (for instance, perhaps they sound alike or look alike) in order to help students remember them.
- Create associations (through silly stories, linking, pairing, or other mnemonic techniques) using vivid imagery, color, and action. Make the imagery as absurd and exaggerated as possible, in order to make it memorable.

- Chunk information that needs to be remembered into small bites. Long series of numbers, such as Social Security numbers and phone numbers, are chunked for that reason.

- Emotional memory is very strong. When you can evoke an emotion while teaching something, it sticks. Teaching through storytelling is a powerful tool because stories evoke emotions in the listener.

- After directions are given, have children repeat the directions back.

- Use visual or graphic depictions to help in remembering routines, procedures, or sequences of steps.

- To help lock information into long-term memory, do something interactive or reflective with the material: discuss it, paraphrase it, write notes about it, or make a story map of it.

- Play memory games in order to build students' skills—for example,

  - *I'm Going on a Trip.* One person says, "I'm going on a trip, and in my suitcase, I'm packing a _____." The next person repeats that line and the item the previous person(s) said in correct sequence, adding a new item at the end to the list. This game helps students to practice auditory sequential memory skills.

  - *Concentration.* Turn up two cards out of an array of several that are facing down, and find matches. This game is good for practicing visual memory skills. This can also be done as a study technique. One of the cards in each pair is the question; the other is the answer.

- Have students flag, tab, or highlight important information in the text to be remembered.

- Encourage students to list as much material as they can remember as fast as possible after instruction, or encourage them to talk it over.

Provide Support for Memory Weaknesses

- Teach students with memory weaknesses to use checklists, task cards, calendars or planners, and other such tools. Help students develop the habit of using planners or calendars on a regular basis in order to remember due dates, tests, after-school activities, and appointments. (See Checklists 3.7 and 4.6.)

- Provide simple written instructions and reminders.

- Supply and use sticky notes for reminders. Encourage students to place them in strategic locations.

- See Checklists 2.4, 2.6, 2.7, 2.8, 4.1, 4.2, and 4.6 for supports and accommodations that teachers can provide in order to strengthen academic areas that are affected by memory weaknesses (for example, learning "sight words," homework, time management, vocabulary, reading comprehension, spelling).

4.8 Strategies for Teaching Reading in the Content Areas

By the time that students reach middle school and high school, there is a significant shift in reading demands. In the elementary grades, reading instruction focuses on mastering skills in decoding, vocabulary, fluency, and comprehension. Students may be grouped according to their reading skill levels in order to receive the extra instruction they need.

Once students move beyond elementary school, content-area courses, such as history and science, are taught by specialty teachers and there may be a wide range of student reading ability in each class. Students are faced with greater quantities of expository (nonfiction, factual) reading. Textbooks and other reading materials may be provided to the entire class, regardless of the individual reading levels of the students. Also, textbooks are often written above grade level. So, a seventh-grade textbook may actually be written at a ninth-grade reading level or even higher. To work effectively with expository texts written at or above grade level, students need to have mastered basic reading skills and have adequate reading fluency. Students with dyslexia are at a considerable disadvantage when working with reading material beyond their skill level.

Teachers in the upper grades may be faced with a broad spectrum of students in their classes, and some of these may require modifications of curriculum and instruction in order to learn the subject material. This situation is especially challenging for teachers who do not have adequate training or materials to teach below-level readers. Fortunately, many schools have learning specialists who can assist in this process. In addition, the use of research-based reading instruction can benefit students of any age and contribute to an increase in their skills. Students with dyslexia may have strong interests in the content areas, so that their motivation contributes to a willingness to read for information, even when that is a difficult process.

Providing students with dyslexia in middle school and high school with continued reading support is necessary so that they can keep up with the curriculum. Some of these students will need continued support in basic reading skills. Most students with dyslexia also need help in learning to derive meaning from expository text.

Effective Teaching in the Content Areas

- Make assistive technology available in the classroom for students with reading and writing disabilities. (See Checklists 2.13 and 2.14.)

- Provide opportunities for active learning (such as science labs) that do not always rely heavily on reading skills.

- Use graphic organizers to help structure learning and to identify important concepts.

- Provide course outlines, class notes, and study guides for students who have difficulty reading independently.

- Consider peer tutoring as a means of assisting students with challenging written material.

- Encourage discussions as a means of creating interest, sharing information, and exploring new material.

- Provide alternative forms of assessment, so that students are not judged by reading and writing skills only.

- Provide extended time for assignments that are reading-intensive in order to accommodate students who read slowly.

- Model reading fluency and expression by reading aloud to students. Modeling expression is especially important in reading plays and other literary works, so that students have an opportunity to hear the importance of inflection, dialect, and emotional expression in reading.

- Work together with your school's reading specialist to determine the readability levels of your class material. A readability formula can be used to identify the difficulty level of different materials. Readability resources are also available at www.micropowerandlight.com/index.html and www .stylewriter-usa.com/readability.html. Teachers should attempt to find differentiated source material so that students at various reading levels have appropriate material to read or teacher-prepared material made available to them.

- Use cooperative learning and differentiated instruction to reach a broad range of students in the classroom.

- Make use of your school's special educators; they can suggest alternative lesson formats, help you modify instructional materials, and suggest modifications in assessment procedures.

- If a student is working with a special educator or tutor, maintain communication so that subject matter can be appropriately modified or taught in different ways during individual or small-group sessions. If a student is having difficulty learning material in the classroom, a special educator or tutor may try to locate other resources to reinforce what was taught or help determine which concepts need review or reteaching on a more individualized level.

- Set up specific times when you are available for questions, clarification of information, and test reviews. Some students prefer to approach teachers this way rather than to ask in front of a large class.

Ways to Help Students with Vocabulary

- Pre-teach new vocabulary words, especially in subjects such as math in which an understanding of technical words is essential.

- Teach students to use context clues to figure out unfamiliar words.

- Point out words that have different meanings in the content area—for example, *reservation*, *roots*, and *base*.

- When introducing new subject vocabulary, use familiar affixes to teach the meaning of new words (for example, *biology, biodegradable, biochemistry*)

- Preview new vocabulary before students read a chapter or article independently. Because reading comprehension is affected by lack of vocabulary knowledge, students with reading problems benefit from knowing as many words as possible prior to reading.

- Provide multiple exposures to new vocabulary words.

- Have students use new words in sentences and activities so that they develop an active understanding of them. (For example, "Workers were considered to be members of the *proletariat*.")

- Use semantic maps to actively involve students in understanding new words. (In a semantic map, a word is placed in the middle, and definitions, examples, synonyms, and related words are written around the edges.)

- For other ideas, see Checklist 2.6.

Ways to Help Students with Comprehension

- Ask questions that help students focus on the important information in a chapter or book.

- Provide a purpose for reading expository text, so that students know what to look for when they read.

- Use prior knowledge to support new information.

- Teach students how to use features of expository texts (for example, headings, indexes, charts, and illustrations) to aid in comprehension.

- Provide students with study guides so that they are able to hold on to the important information from their reading.

- Students need additional opportunities to explore concepts introduced in their textbooks. Use hands-on activities to help reinforce what they have read. For example, teach students how to plan a healthy menu the day after they read about nutrition.

- When possible, provide additional reading material that is easier to read for students who are reading below grade level.

- Encourage students who read below grade level to listen to audio versions of books and textbooks (see Checklist 2.13). For some students, this is an effective way to absorb new information.

- Teach students to periodically (perhaps every page or every chapter) take notes and summarize what they have read. When they keep a running summary as they read, they can review the important points after they finish. This practice works well for both narrative and expository text.

- Encourage re-reading as a means of deriving greater meaning.

- Provide students with opportunities to discuss in small groups what they have read. This activity serves as another way for weak readers to gain some of the information they may have missed.

- Use graphic organizers and concept maps to help visually explain new concepts and information. Many resources on graphic organizers are available at www.sdcoe.k12.ca.us/score/actbank/torganiz.htm and www.graphic.org.

- See Checklist 2.7 for more comprehension strategies.

Resources

Division for Learning Disabilities & Division for Research of the Council for Exceptional Children. (2001, Summer). *Current practice alerts: A focus on mnemonic instruction.* Issue 5. Retrieved from www.dldcec .org/alerts

Lapp, D., Flood, J., & Farnan, N. (2004). *Content area reading and learning.* Mahwah, NJ: Routledge.

Rief, S. (2003). *The ADHD book of lists: A practical guide for helping children and teens with attention deficit disorders.* San Francisco: Jossey-Bass.

Rief, S. (2005). *How to reach and teach children with ADD/ADHD* (2nd ed.). San Francisco: Jossey-Bass.

Rief, S. (2008). *The ADD/ADHD checklist A practical reference for parents and teachers* (2nd ed.). San Francisco: Jossey-Bass.

Rief, S., & Heimburge, J. (2006). *How to reach and teach all children in the inclusive classroom* (2nd ed.). San Francisco: Jossey-Bass.

Stone, R. (2002). *Best practices for high school classrooms: What award-winning secondary teachers do.* Thousand Oaks, CA: Corwin Press.

5

OTHER IMPORTANT CHECKLISTS FOR PARENTS AND TEACHERS

Introduction

High school and college students with dyslexia face many challenges. They benefit greatly when educators and parents share useful strategies and suggestions to help guide them.

Response to Intervention (RtI) is a process for identifying students grades K–12 in need of academic and behavioral support. The goal is to prevent children from falling through the cracks by providing tiers of intervention within the general education program that are matched to students' needs.

This section provides information about special education law, the educational rights of students with dyslexia, and how RtI is used as part of the process for identifying students with learning disabilities who qualify for special education.

5.1 High School Students with Dyslexia

By the time they reach high school, students who have been diagnosed with dyslexia may have received additional help with reading and writing skills for many years. However, problems with phonological processing often continue to make reading, writing, and spelling difficult at a time when demands of the curriculum increase considerably.

Students with dyslexia face most of the same academic requirements, high-stakes testing, and social complexities as their high school peers while also coping with a disability. Adolescents with dyslexia will usually benefit from additional support, although it may not always be welcomed by them. Parents and teachers may find it challenging to find a reasonable balance between giving teenagers sufficient guidance and encouraging independence and self-advocacy skills.

Students diagnosed with dyslexia for the first time in high school will need many opportunities to catch up on missing skills. It is not too late to improve the reading and writing skills of high school students who continue to have reading problems. Many techniques and commercial remedial materials for older students can be used quite effectively to strengthen reading skills of adolescents.

Reading researchers have shown that older students with reading deficits benefit from systematic, intensive small-group work on decoding, phonological skills, vocabulary, comprehension practice, and instruction in the use of specific reading strategies. Work on reading fluency becomes especially important in high school because students are expected to manage large amounts of reading for many of their classes.

In the content areas, teachers can provide valuable support in reading comprehension and vocabulary development. Providing students with advance graphic organizers that present the main concepts that will be found in the reading helps students derive more from the text. For other ideas, see Checklists 2.6, 2.7, and 4.8.

Making technology available to students with dyslexia can help ease some of their difficulties—for example, having computers available for writing tasks or providing online teacher notes to students. For other suggestions see Checklist 2.13.

Individualized Education Programs (IEPs) for high school students with dyslexia should contain goals that are specific to their individual problems with reading and written language. If a student has weaknesses in basic reading skills, vocabulary, comprehension, writing mechanics, or expression, those should be addressed in his or her IEP objectives. Goals that address specific needs in specific subjects and in study skills should be included.

By the time a student is sixteen years old, plans for transition services should also become part of the IEP. The IEP team looks at what the student intends to do after high school—perhaps get a higher education or enter the job market. Transition plans address needs such as preparation for college entrance examinations, consideration of career choices, development of extracurricular interests, and job training possibilities. See Checklist 5.5.

Recommendations for High School Students with Dyslexia

- Before reading a textbook chapter, look over chapter and section headings. Scan for unfamiliar words. Find definitions so that they will make sense when you come to them in your reading.

- Spread out large reading assignments. When possible, divide up sections of reading so that you can do some each day. If that is not possible, read a section at a time, then take a short break before you continue. This method will help you reduce fatigue and get more out of what you are reading.

- Highlight or take notes as you read so that you stay focused. Speak into an audio recorder if this is easier than writing notes.

- When you read, ask yourself, "Does this make sense?" If not, you may need to re-read, look up vocabulary words, or ask for help with the material.
- Write a short summary after every page or two when you are reading.
- Outside of school, try to read regularly. Doing so will help you improve your vocabulary and reading skills. Choose books on subjects that interest you, so that you will be more motivated to do the reading.
- Use a PDA or calendar to record due dates of projects and long-term assignments and dates of tests, appointments, and special events. Get in the habit of checking daily to see what you need to take care of. Talk with your teachers about ways you might be able to access their lectures, if you missed a lecture, or in case you need additional opportunities to listen to what they said in class. (See Checklist 4.3 for various ways teachers might provide students this access if they are willing to do so.)
- Find out when your teachers are available outside of class time to answer questions, help with test preparation, or provide you with missing assignments. If you are having difficul-ties in a class, make sure to talk with the teacher, so that you can work together to figure out what to do.
- Get to know your guidance counselor. He or she can help keep teachers informed about your educational needs and monitor how things are going in your classes. In your junior year (or before), your counselor can help you begin to think about your plans after high school.
- If you will be taking college entrance exams (SAT, ACT), discuss with your parents whether you should take a preparation class, work with a tutor, or devise your own study plan. If you are entitled to extended time for testing (or other test accommodations), work with your counselor and parents to get the necessary documentation in on time.

- If you are a student who does better when working orally rather than in writing, make an effort to participate regularly in class discussions, so that you can demonstrate to your teachers that you understand the material.

- Use study guides provided by teachers when you prepare for tests. Fill them in over a period of days so that they do not become too overwhelming.

- Make it a habit to read directions carefully. Look them over several times. Highlight important words (such as "show your work" in math or "circle the correct answer.")

- Edit your work before handing it in. Doing work on a computer makes it easier to check over and to save.

- Attend your IEP meetings with your parent (or parents). Take the opportunity to discuss what you need in your high school classes in order to help you learn in the best way possible. Share concerns and problems that need to be worked out.

5.2 College Students with Dyslexia

Students with dyslexia can be found in all postsecondary education programs. Some students choose to spend part or all of their college years in programs that specialize in teaching students with disabilities. Many more students with dyslexia, however, successfully complete mainstream colleges and graduate school programs. They do so by effectively using the supports available through modern technology, accessing school support programs, working closely with their professors, and making use of their own advocacy and coping skills. Disability support departments, sometimes known as *learning support services*, are now common in higher education institutions, from community colleges through graduate schools.

The Americans with Disabilities Act ensures that students with disabilities can receive reasonable accommodations in private and public colleges and universities. Higher education institutions are expected to make necessary adaptations so that students can take part in classes, activities, and tests without being penalized for their disabilities. Students with disabilities are entitled to the same access to programs as their peers.

Students with disabilities are responsible for letting their school know about their disabilities by submitting records of high school IEPs, 504 plans, and evaluations, so that appropriate accommodations will be provided and instructors will be notified about specific student needs. Schools have the right to determine which accommodations a student is entitled to, based on their interpretation of that student's documentation.

Recommendations for College Students with Dyslexia

- Get to know the disability support services available at your college. Check to see what types of support services are offered when you are applying to colleges, to see whether the schools are able to provide the assistance you need.

Make an appointment when you plan to visit the campus so that you can learn about all available services.

- Before registering for your freshman year, make sure to let your school know about your disability and provide copies of any documentation you have.

- Take advantage of services offered by your school, such as peer tutoring, mentoring, study skills programs, and test-taking workshops. Talk with your professors about ways you might be able to access their lectures, if you missed a lecture, or in case you need additional opportunities to listen to what they said in class. (See Checklist 4.3 for various ways instructors might provide students with this access if they are willing to do so.)

- Check in with the disability support staff throughout the year rather than just when you have a problem.

- Consult your college advisor when deciding on a course load each semester. A student with dyslexia should avoid taking too many courses during one semester that demand large amounts of reading.

- Consider taking one fewer course each semester and planning to graduate one or two semesters later. This strategy is especially beneficial during freshman year.

- If you have not been diagnosed with a learning disability, even though you may have had a history of academic difficulties, you may find it very useful to have a psycho-educational evaluation early in your college career (or the year prior to college), to obtain a more concise view of your learning issues. College counseling centers and disability support programs are good sources of referrals to professionals who test young adults for learning problems.

- If your reading skills are still weak by the end of high school, consider taking a developmental reading course during the first year of college if available at your school to strengthen your reading skills. You can also take such a class during the summer prior to entering college.

- Take advantage of support services at your college. Some community colleges and four-year colleges offer summer study skills classes to help students prepare for college. Many colleges have writing centers where students are given individualized assistance with organizing, writing, and editing their work. Math labs and computer labs may also be available.

- Use strategies for decoding, comprehension, and fluency to get the most from college reading assignments. (See Checklists 2.3, 2.5, 2.7.)

- Consider working once or twice a week with a professional tutor who can provide individualized help in your areas of weakness (for example, reading, study skills, or math).

- If you had a 504 plan or *an IEP* in high school, similar accommodations may be available at the college level. Such accommodations may include modifications in testing, extended time for tests and assignments, or a designated note taker. Discuss these issues with the disability support staff at your college.

- Identify good places to study on campus. A dorm room may be too distracting, especially if you have reading and concentration problems.

- If you are eligible to use audio books, check to see whether any of the ones you need are available through the campus library or through interlibrary loan. Before the semester begins, find out from professors which books you will need so that you have enough time to order them.

- Check into the organizations Recording for the Blind and Dyslexic and Bookshare, which provide digitally recorded textbooks and other written material to eligible reading disabled students. (See Checklist 2.13.)

- Consider forming or joining study groups when preparing for tests. Study groups are a good way to review what has been read and learn from others.

- Students who know how to advocate for themselves or who learn to do so will be able to collaborate better with their teachers in order to let them know how to help most effectively. While college professors may not be specifically trained to teach students with dyslexia, many are willing to listen to what a student needs and make adjustments that help. Take advantage of professors' office hours to explain in detail what your disability means, your needs, and what kinds of accommodations you are entitled to receive.

- Take advantage of technology such as Kurzweil software and audio books. Get to know the resources that are available on campus, such as services for computer advice and repair. (See Checklist 2.13.)

- Improve your keyboarding skills before going to college. This step will help reduce the stress of writing papers.

- Before leaving home, make sure to have plans in place for handling these issues at school:
    - Medication refills (if needed)
    - A budget for expenses
    - A system for storing papers, books, the syllabus for each course, and notebooks
    - A way to record (and check) dates and times for classes, appointments, and social events
    - A plan for accessing audio books, if you need them

5.3 Response to Intervention

Response to Intervention (RtI) is

- A multi-tiered instructional approach that focuses on problem prevention and early identification of students who are not progressing at the same rate as their peers, and provides evidence-based interventions at increasing levels of intensity to those at risk of academic failure
- A schoolwide process that provides systematic, evidence-based instruction and a continuum of intervention tiers to struggling learners
- A single, integrated system of instruction and intervention aimed at improving educational outcomes for *all* students and guided by data on student outcomes from frequent progress-monitoring measures
- The practice of providing high-quality instruction and research-based interventions matched to students' needs, and using individual students' response to those interventions to make a range of educational decisions—including part of the process to determine whether a student qualifies for special education
- A general education initiative that is written into the special education law IDEA 2004 and that offers a framework for structuring early intervention services (EIS) that can replace the traditional model of examining discrepancies between intelligence and achievement to identify students with learning disabilities eligible for special education.

Essential Components of RtI

- High-quality, research-based instruction for all students, differentiated to match their learning needs
- Universal screening of all students early in the school year and repeated during the year, to identify students at risk for academic or behavioral failure

- Implementation of scientifically proven interventions to address students' learning problems
- Administration of interventions by highly qualified personnel in accordance with the programs' instructions and protocol
- Multiple, increasingly intense tiers of intervention
- Continual monitoring of students' performance and response to interventions
- Educational decisions about individual students based on solid assessment data and monitoring of student progress
- Parental involvement and team-based decision making in regard to a student's educational needs

The Three-Tiered Model of Intervention

School districts vary in their implementation of tiered intervention models. Most common is the three-tiered model of academic and behavioral supports and interventions, represented as a pyramid divided into three sections. The largest section and bottom part of the pyramid (about 80 percent of students) represents Tier I. A smaller section in the middle of the pyramid (about 15 percent) represents Tier II. The small part at the top (about 5 percent) represents Tier III.

Tier I: Primary Intervention
- Tier I focuses on taking a proactive approach, aiming to prevent problems by identifying at-risk students and catching students in need of support before they fail.
- High-quality, research-based instruction in the core curriculum and effective management and behavioral supports are provided by classroom teachers.
- Effective strategies and differentiated instruction provided at this tier should allow approximately 80 percent of students to achieve academically at expected levels.

- Screening, regular assessment, progress monitoring, and group interventions are provided for all students.
- Identified at-risk students receive additional instruction within the general education classroom for a period of time, during which progress is closely monitored, data are collected, and the need for Tier II intervention is determined.

Tier II: Targeted Secondary Intervention

- Tier II involves more intense, targeted interventions to strengthen the skills of students who do not respond adequately with Tier I support.
- Research-based interventions are provided *in addition to* core instruction in the general curriculum, usually in small groups. This is supplemental instruction that does not replace the classroom curriculum.
- Tier II will be the appropriate level of support for approximately 15 percent of the school population, enabling those students to be successful.
- Tier II interventions are applied for a limited time (generally no more than ten to twelve weeks), during which students' progress is frequently monitored in order to gauge the effectiveness of the intervention and determine whether Tier III intervention is needed.

Tier III: Tertiary Intervention

- In Tier III, intensive, individualized interventions target the skill deficits of students who do not adequately respond to intervention in Tiers I and II.
- Students at Tier III receive the most minutes of instruction, delivered by teachers who are well trained to implement the intervention programs.
- Tier III is the stage at which children are considered for special education.

- In some school districts, Tier III is when referral for special education and evaluation takes place. (Documented evidence of lack of response to intervention at Tiers I and II is a component of the evaluation.) For students who are found to be eligible for special education, Tier III intervention consists of special education services.

- In other districts, a more intensive, individualized Tier III intervention is provided for a limited period of time within general education, generally delivered by reading specialists or other specialists. Referral and evaluation for special education follows if the student does not make adequate progress. In these districts, special education is Tier IV.

RtI and Special Education Law

- When the Individuals with Disabilities Education Act (the U.S. special education law) was reauthorized in 2004, it changed the way that school districts are permitted to evaluate and identify students with learning disabilities.

- Traditionally, a formula that quantified the discrepancy between a student's intelligence and his or her achievement was used to determine whether a student had a learning disability and qualified for special education.

- There have been problems with the intelligence-achievement discrepancy formula. Concerns about requiring its use in the diagnosis of learning disabilities and determination of eligibility for special education have been expressed by many. For example,

  - Questions have been raised about the formula's reliability in diagnosis; many reasons might underlie a student's underachievement, not necessarily a learning disability.

  - The fact that many students must wait until they fail in order to be found eligible for special education is problematic.

- IDEA 2004 allows RtI to be used as part of the process of determining whether a student has specific learning disabilities and is eligible for special education.
- The law stresses the need to utilize instructional practices in general education that are supported by research and that focus on prevention of problems. "Early intervening services" (EIS) are to be provided to help students who are not yet identified as eligible for special education, but who require additional academic or behavioral support.
- According to IDEA 2004, a student who consistently performs below state-approved grade-level standards on scientifically validated interventions and fails to respond successfully to additional supports and interventions of increasing intensity may be determined to have a learning disability.
- In 2006, the U.S. Department of Education issued regulations that provided clarification and guidance to states and school districts about how to implement IDEA 2004 and RtI.
- The regulations specify that
  - Schools must provide early intervention to struggling learners in general education, delivered by highly qualified personnel.
  - Data-based documentation of repeated assessments at reasonable intervals must be collected and used to guide educational decisions through a problem-solving approach.
  - The RtI process is encouraged (in lieu of the intelligence-achievement discrepancy formula) as one component of a comprehensive evaluation for the purpose of identifying students with learning disabilities and for determining special education eligibility.
  - To identify a student as having a learning disability, it must be determined that the low achievement is not due

to the student's lack of appropriate instruction in general education.

- If frequent monitoring of progress and data-based documentation show that a student is still not making adequate progress after receiving research-based instruction and intervention, a referral for testing is appropriate.

Benefits of RtI for Students with Dyslexia

When implemented effectively, RtI has many benefits for students, particularly those with reading disabilities. RtI can

- Significantly reduce academic failure and behavioral problems, increasing the success of many students within general education.

- Reduce the time that a student waits before receiving additional instructional assistance. Early intervention is critical to educational outcomes for children who are learning to read.

- Reduce inappropriate or unnecessary special education referrals and placements.

- Increase the quality of instruction and the use of research-validated practices in general education classrooms.

- *Prevent* reading disabilities and subsequent years of school failure and loss of self-esteem by providing scientifically based instruction and early intervention.

- Ensure that general education assumes responsibility for all children (including those with disabilities) and provides the degree of support and intervention that individual students need for success. No longer should a struggling reader need to qualify for special education in order to receive supplementary reading instruction to improve skills, nor do children need to wait until they lag behind grade-level peers so that even with intensive remediation they cannot catch up.

- Prevent some children with dyslexia and other learning disabilities from requiring special education because the research-based instruction and supports within general education sufficiently meet their needs.
- Provide close monitoring and documentation of student progress with prereferral interventions.
- Reduce some unnecessary and time-consuming testing from the evaluation process.

Potential Disadvantages of RtI for Students with Dyslexia

There are also some potential problems and disadvantages with RtI, particularly in the diagnostic process for determining if a student has a specific learning disability. Parents and educators need to know that

- The law does not address how children should be evaluated when they do not respond to the interventions.
- There is ambiguity about the components of a comprehensive evaluation under this model (as opposed to the traditional discrepancy model) for determining the presence of learning disabilities.
- The effectiveness of a school's implementation of RtI requires the designated staff (well-trained in the research-based methods) for providing the intervention programs. Not every school will have the availability of these teachers or other "highly qualified personnel" to implement the interventions. Consequently, the success of the RtI model may vary from school to school.
- There is minimal information or research to support the RtI model for students in grades higher than elementary level.

- There are no timelines in the law for how long students should receive interventions in RtI tiers before they are referred for testing. These are decisions at the local level. However, it is important to know that a referral for special education and a comprehensive evaluation may be made at any time in the RtI process. Parents need to be informed of their rights to request such a referral for evaluation regardless of where the student is in the RtI process.

5.4 Special Education

The Individuals with Disabilities Education Act (IDEA) is the federal special education law that protects the educational rights of students with disabilities. This law has been in effect since 1975, and it has been amended by Congress numerous times over the years. IDEA was reauthorized in 2004 and became effective the following year. The U.S. Department of Education issued regulations in 2006, which provide clarification to states and school districts about how to implement IDEA.

Special education refers to "specially designed instruction," which is instruction designed to meet the individual needs of the child with a disability. Special education and related services for students with disabilities are provided at no cost to parents.

IDEA includes rules and requirements for appropriate specially designed instruction and related services to children with disabilities.

IDEA states that a student with a disability who requires special education or related services is entitled to a free appropriate public education in the least restrictive environment. The following relates to the rights of all special education students who receive services through the public schools:

- An Individualized Education Program (IEP), tailored to the specific needs of the individual student, must be developed for each student who is classified with a disability and who meets eligibility criteria for special education and related services. See Checklist 5.5 for more information about the IEP.
- All decisions on special education services and placements are made together by the student's parents and the local school district, known as the local education agency (LEA).
- A number of rules, regulations, procedural safeguards, and timelines govern the referral and IEP process, and districts are required by law to follow them. Many state laws and

rules go beyond the requirements of IDEA. Parents should become familiar with disability laws in their own state, because there is some variance among states.

- There are different categories of disabilities. Dyslexia falls under the category of specific learning disability (SLD). See Checklist 1.1 for a discussion of the definition of a learning disability.

- Students with disabilities may also be entitled to "related services," depending on their specific needs and coexisting conditions. Related services may include social work services, speech-language therapy, occupational therapy, special transportation, and others.

- Not all students with disabilities, including those who have dyslexia or other learning disabilities, are found eligible for special education.

- Once a student is provided with a comprehensive multidisciplinary evaluation, the IEP team determines whether he or she has a disability that impairs learning or other areas of functioning and for which special education and related services are needed. IDEA requires that the disability adversely affects the student's educational performance in order for the student to qualify for special education. *The law does not require that a student have failed courses or been retained a grade* in order to be eligible for special education.

- Parent Training and Information Centers are useful resources to contact in order to learn more about special education and related services. Many state laws and rules go beyond the requirements of IDEA.

- Parents of students with disabilities should be aware of their children's rights under the law.

- If parents feel that their child's educational rights are not being upheld, they have a right to file a due process complaint with their local school district. An impartial hearing officer hears these cases.

The Referral Process for Special Education

- Parents or school staff members may initiate a referral for an evaluation or consideration for special education services for their child.
- Requests for evaluation should be made in writing to the school or district (usually to the principal or director of special education). It is recommended that the explanation include why the student may need special education services.
- Students in public schools and charter schools are referred for special education programs through the schools they attend.
- Parents must give written consent for their child to be evaluated.
- Schools collect information on students who are not making satisfactory progress in academic areas (such as reading) from elementary grades through high school. Information should be obtained from students' records, from classroom observations, and from parents and teachers. Results from vision and hearing screenings, standardized and curriculum-based assessments, and other relevant sources should also be considered.
- The interdisciplinary team that helps determine whether a child has a learning disability (such as dyslexia) may include
    - Parents
    - School administrator
    - School psychologist
    - Classroom teacher
    - Special education teacher
    - Speech-language pathologist, reading teacher, and other school professionals or specialists
- As described in Checklist 5.3, Response to Intervention (RtI) is a process that is used in many districts to determine

whether a student meets the necessary criteria for participation in special education under the category of specific
learning disabilities. At any stage of the RtI process, parents
and school staff have the right to refer a student for special
education evaluation.

- In an RtI setting, the local education agency (LEA) may
use a process that determines whether a child responds to
research-based intervention as a part of the evaluation procedure. (See Checklist 5.3.)

Provision of Services

- School districts and states vary in their procedures for
considering eligibility for special education and in the
types of programs and services provided to students with
disabilities.

- Most students with dyslexia and other learning disabilities
who qualify for special education are taught in general education classrooms, receiving the services of a special education teacher directly in their classroom or pulled out (usually
in small groups) in a resource room or learning center setting for part of the day.

- Some students with learning disabilities are placed in "special day classes" where they receive instruction from the
special education teacher for most of the day and are
integrated with general education students for part of
the day.

- In order to identify reading concerns early, many school
districts administer assessments to young students to determine who is at risk of reading difficulties. Students who are
at risk can then be placed into intensive reading instruction
programs within the general education program. Students
who respond to this instruction may not require subsequent
special education placement.

- Early identification and prompt service delivery are considered the most effective ways to begin to help students with academic problems and possible disabilities.
- Students who do not respond well to the tiered process of RtI are then considered for special education programs. See Checklist 5.3.

Provision of Services for Students Who Attend Private and Parochial Schools

- While private and parochial schools are not required to provide special education services, parents of students who are attending such schools may request a referral for testing and special education services through the local public school system in which the student lives.
- The LEA determines whether children who are attending private schools should be evaluated through the public school system. Parents contact their local Office of Special Education to get the local office involved in looking at a student for possible evaluation for placement in a special education program in their local public school.
- The LEA may decide to do an evaluation and write an IEP if a disability is identified and the student meets the criteria for special education and related services. However, public school systems and private schools are not mandated to carry out the IEP if the student does not attend a public school.
- If a private school student is found to have a learning disability by the LEA and is entitled to special education and related services, the parent may have to transport the child to the local public school to receive the specialized instruction and recommended services. If a parent chooses instead to obtain specialized instruction and services privately, the LEA may provide some level of reimbursement for certain eligible services.

5.5 Individualized Education Plans

When a student is found to be eligible for special education services, an Individualized Education Program (IEP) is written. An IEP is a written plan created to meet a student's specific learning and behavioral needs. Learning goals are developed with a focus on educating students within the general education program as much as possible. All special education and related services to be provided to the student are included in the IEP.

The IEP is developed by the school IEP team and the student's parents, who, ideally, make a coordinated effort in educating the student with a disability. The IEP serves as a means of accountability for those delivering services to the student.

- An IEP describes
  - Annual goals for the student
  - The student's present level of performance in academic, developmental, and other areas of functioning
  - Results of evaluations of the student
  - Strengths of the student
  - How the student's disability affects his or her learning and participation in the general education program
  - Special education programs and related services the student is to receive
  - Where and by whom the services are to be delivered
  - Frequency of services to be delivered
  - How annual progress goals will be measured
  - Modifications to be made in assessments, if any are deemed necessary, for example, writing directly in the test booklet
  - Transition goals and services that must be in place no later than by the time the student is sixteen years of age.

These are education and training goals to help students with disabilities make a transition to work or further education and independent living after high school.

- IEP annual goals
  - Must be clearly stated and objectively measurable
  - Should be specific to the student's needs
  - Describe the skills and behaviors that the student is expected to learn
  - Help guide instruction for the student
- A student may be invited to attend IEP meetings that pertain to him or her. (Parents are consulted before the student is invited.)
- Parents are an important part of the team that develops the IEP. They provide input and share concerns about their child and his or her needs. They also must be informed of their child's progress on IEP goals during the year.
- Parents should receive a copy of their child's IEP at the end of the IEP meeting.
- A student's IEP goals should be shared with all teachers who are expected to help carry out the goals for that student, and each person's role should be clearly defined.
- Each IEP is reviewed and revised as needed (at least annually) by the school's multidisciplinary team and the student's parents.
- Parents and members of the IEP team may request more frequent meetings for IEP reviews and revisions. Parents must be invited to all of these meetings.
- Students are entitled to re-evaluations every three years unless parents and the LEA agree that a re-evaluation is not necessary at that time.

- If a student with an IEP moves to a different school district, a new IEP may be written. Otherwise, the new district follows the IEP from the previous district.

- If an IEP meeting is held for a student who attends a private school, the school is invited to send a representative to attend the meeting.

5.6 Section 504

In addition to IDEA, there are other laws that protect people with disabilities against discrimination:

- Section 504 of the Rehabilitation Act of 1973 (known as *Section 504*)
- Americans with Disabilities Act (ADA) Amendments Act of 2008

Section 504 is a civil rights statute that prohibits discrimination and is enforced by the U.S. Office of Civil Rights. It is not funded, and school districts receive no financial assistance for implementing it. Section 504 protects people with disabilities against discrimination and applies to any agency that receives federal funding, which includes all public schools and many private schools. Children who qualify for services under IDEA eligibility criteria are automatically covered under Section 504. However, the reverse is not true. See Checklists 5.4 and 5.5.

The ADA Amendments Act of 2008 made significant changes to the ADA of 1990 that have a direct impact on Section 504 and how it affects students with learning disabilities, including dyslexia, ADHD, and other mild to moderate disabilities.

These two civil rights statutes (Section 504 and ADA 2008) are interpreted together, so as of 2009, the amendments to ADA apply to Section 504's rules, definition of who has a disability, eligibility criteria, and other factors.

Section 504 require School districts to provide students with disabilities with the following:

- A free and appropriate public education in the least restrictive environment with their nondisabled peers to the maximum extent appropriate to their individual needs

- Supports (adaptations, accommodations, modifications, and related aids and services) to allow each student an equal opportunity to participate and learn in the general education program
- The opportunity to participate in extracurricular and non-academic activities
- A free, nondiscriminatory evaluation
- Procedural due process

Eligibility Criteria under Section 504

- Children with learning disabilities such as dyslexia, ADHD, or others with disabilities who do not qualify for special education under IDEA may be eligible to receive accommodations and supplementary and related aids and services under a Section 504 plan.
- Section 504 protects students if they fit the following criteria:
  - The student has a record of or is regarded as having a physical or mental impairment.
  - The physical or mental impairment substantially limits one or more major life activities.

Changes to Section 504 as of ADA 2008

There have been significant changes to Section 504 eligibility criteria as of the ADA Amendments Act of 2008. These include

- "Major life activity" has been expanded to include, among a number of other things, "learning, reading, concentrating, thinking, communicating, working." In consideration of physical impairments, "major bodily functions" have been expanded to include neurological and brain functions.

- Language was added: "An impairment that is episodic or in remission is a disability if it would substantially limit a major life activity when active." So the limitation of a major life activity doesn't need to be constant.

- "Mitigating measures" can no longer be used when evaluating whether a person has a disability (except for the use of contact lenses or glasses that correct a vision problem). Mitigating measures, which offset the effects of an impairment, include, among other things, medication, hearing aids, and learning adaptations (such as assistive technology or accommodations).

- Schools must now evaluate under Section 504 without considering the impact of these mitigating measures (for example, a student's use of medication, recorded books, reading assistance, or extra time on tests) in determining whether a student has a disability.

- These changes will undoubtedly enable more people with dyslexia and other disabilities to be eligible for Section 504 accommodation plans than have been eligible in the past. For students with dyslexia, who may not qualify for an IEP, a 504 plan can certainly be beneficial.

504 Accommodations

Section 504 plans include some accommodations that are deemed most important for a student to have an equal opportunity to be successful at school. They do not include everything that might be helpful for a student but include only reasonable supports and accommodations that will enable opportunities to learn that are commensurate with those of a student's nondisabled peers. Accommodations are primarily the responsibility of the teacher (or teachers) and other general education school staff. Following are some examples of possible 504 plan accommodations:

- Preferential seating
- Enlarged or modified texts
- Extra review or assistance
- Breaking long-term projects and work assignments into shorter tasks
- Audio recordings of books
- Copies of class notes from a designated note taker
- Reduced homework assignments
- Extended time on tests
- Assistance with organization of materials and work space
- Access to a calculator for math computation
- Access to a computer or portable word processor for written work
- A peer buddy to clarify directions
- A peer tutor
- Use of daily and weekly notes or a monitoring form between home and school for communication

More guidance will be provided in the months and years ahead in regard to the interpretation of Section 504 provisions in accordance with the ADA Amendments Act of 2008. See the Web sites on disability in Checklist 5.7 and the resources at the end of this section for more information.

5.7 National Organizations and Resources That Address Disability Issues

The following Web sites are listed alphabetically in each category. In addition to these, several Web sites that offer information and resources on numerous topics are mentioned in checklists throughout this book and at the end of each section.

Organizations and Resources That Address Learning Disabilities

- Academic Language Therapy Association (ALTA)
  www.altaread.org
- Alliance for Technology Access
  www.ataccess.org
- Association of Educational Therapists
  www.aetonline.org
- Council for Exceptional Children
  www.cec.sped.org
- Council for Learning Disabilities
  www.cldinternational.org
- Dyslexia Awareness and Resource Center
  www.dyslexiacenter.org
- Family Center on Technology and Disability
  www.fctd.info
- Great Schools (formerly Schwab Learning)
  www.greatschools.net
- The Institute for Multi-Sensory Education (IMSE)
  http://www.orton-gillingham.com
- International Dyslexia Association (formerly Orton Dyslexia Society)
  www.interdys.org
- Internet Resources for Special Children
  http://irsc.org

- LD Online
  www.ldonline.org
- LD Resources
  www.ldresources.org
- Learning Disabilities Worldwide
  www.ldworldwide.org
- Learning Disability Association of America
  www.ldanatl.org
- National Association for the Education of African
  American Children with Learning Disabilities
  www.aacld.org
- National Center for Learning Disabilities
  www.ncld.org
- National Information Clearinghouse for Handicapped
  Children and Youth (also referred to as the
  National Dissemination Center for Children with
  Disabilities)
  www.nichcy.org/
- National Institute of Child Health and Human
  Development
  www.nichd.nih.gov
- National Research Center on Learning Disabilities
  www.nrcld.org/
- Recordings for the Blind and Dyslexic
  www.rfbd.org
- TeachingLD (a service of the Division for Learning
  Disabilities of the Council for Exceptional Children)
  www.teachingld.org
- U.S. Department of Education
  www.ed.gov/parents/needs/speced/resources.html

Children with dyslexia often have coexisting disorders, such as ADHD or speech and language disorders. Some resources on these disorders include these:

- American Speech-Language-Hearing Association
  www.asha.org
- Children and Adults with Attention Deficit Disorder
  www.chadd.org
- National Resource Center on AD/HD, a clearinghouse for science-based information
  www.help4adhd.org

See Checklist 1.11 for organizations that serve twice exceptional children (gifted children with learning disabilities).

Organizations and Resources That Address Educational Rights for Children with Disabilities

- Council of Parent Attorneys and Advocates
  www.copaa.org
- Family and Advocates Partnership for Education
  www.fape.org
- IDEA Partnership
  www.ideapartnership.org
- Monahan and Cohen
  www.monahan-cohen.com
- National Disability Rights Network
  www.ndrn.org
- Parent Advocacy Coalition for Educational Rights (PACER Center)
  www.pacer.org

- Parent Training and Information Centers
  www.taalliance.org
- Reed Martin, Esq.
  www.reedmartin.com
- U.S. Department of Education (on IDEA 2004)
  http://idea.ed.gov
- Wrightslaw
  www.wrightslaw.com

See Section Two for centers and resources on reading research.

Resources

Arieta, C. (2006). *What is reading comprehension and how does it relate to college learning?* Retrieved from Landmark College Institute for Research and Training Web site: http://www.landmark.edu/institute/assistive_technology/reading_overview.html

Casbarro, J. (2008). *Response to intervention.* Port Chester, NY: National Professional Resources.

Cohen, M. (2009). *A guide to special education advocacy: What parents, clinicians and advocates need to know.* Philadelphia: Kingsley.

Curtis, M. B. (2002). *Adolescent reading: A synthesis of research.* Boston: Lesley College, The Center for Special Education.

Deshler, D. D., & Schumaker, J. B. (2006). *Teaching adolescents with disabilities: Accessing the general education curriculum.* Thousand Oaks, CA: Corwin Press.

Gordon, M., & Keiser, S. (Eds.). (1998). *Accommodations in higher education under the Americans with Disabilities Act (ADA): A no-nonsense guide for clinicians, educators, administrators, and lawyers.* DeWitt, NY: GSI.

Heller, R., & Greenleaf, C. L. (2007). *Literacy instruction in the content areas: Getting to the core of middle and high school improvement.* Washington, DC: Alliance for Excellent Education.

International Dyslexia Association. (2007, Fall). A parent's guide to Response-to-Intervention. Retrieved from http://www.abcadvocacy.net/ABC%20FAQ%20208.htm

International Reading Association. (2006). *Standards for middle and high school literacy coaches.* Newark, DE: International Reading Association.

IRIS Center. (2007). *The IRIS Center dialogue guides.* (Materials created by the IRIS Center for the National Association of State Directors of Special Education's IDEA Partnership). Retrieved from http://iris.peabody.vanderbilt.edu/resources.html

Kamil, M. L. (2003). *Adolescents and literacy: Reading for the 21st century.* Washington, DC: Alliance for Excellent Education.

Learning Disabilities Association of America. (May 2006). *Responsiveness to intervention: Questions parents must ask.* Retrieved from the Learning Disabilities Association of America Web site: www.ldanatl.org/news/print_response.asp

McGahee-Kovac, M. (2002). *A student's guide to the IEP.* Retrieved from the National Dissemination Center for Children with Disabilities Web site: http://www.nichcy.org/stuguid.asp

McGahee-Kovac, M. (2002). *A student's guide to the IEP.* Retrieved from http://www.ldonline.org/article/A_Student's_Guide_to_the_IEP/5944

Mooney, J., & Cole, D. (2000). *Learning outside the lines: Two Ivy League students with learning disabilities and ADHD give you the tools for academic success and educational revolution.* New York: Simon & Schuster.

National Center for Learning Disabilities. (www.ld.org). (2006). *A parent's guide to response-to-intervention.* Retrieved from www.ecac-parent-center.org/education/documents/Parents_Guide_to_RTI_000.pdf

Nist, S. L., & Holschuh, J. (2000). *Active learning strategies for college success.* Boston: Allyn & Bacon.

Peterson, C. L., Caverly, D. C., Nicholson, S. A., O'Neal, S., & Cusenbary, S. (2001). *Building reading proficiency at the secondary level.* Austin, TX: Southwest Educational Development Laboratory.

Peterson's. (2007). *Colleges for students with learning disabilities or AD/HD.* Lawrenceville, NJ: Peterson's Guides.

Reiff, H. B. (2007). *Self-advocacy skills for students with learning disabilities: Making it happen in college and beyond.* Port Chester, NY: Dude.

Rief, S. (2008). *The ADD/ADHD checklist: A practical reference for parents and teachers.* San Francisco: Jossey-Bass.

Schoenbach, R., Greenleaf, C., Cziko, C., & Hurwitz, L. (1999). *Reading for understanding: A guide to improving reading in middle and high school classrooms.* San Francisco: Jossey-Bass.

Scholastic. (2005). *The compendium of Read 180 research: 1999–2004.* New York: Scholastic Books.

Siegel, L. (2007). *The complete IEP guide: How to advocate for your special ed child.* Berkeley, CA: Nolo Press

Siegel, L. (2007). *Nolo's IEP guide: Learning disabilities.* Berkeley, CA: Nolo Press.

Staff Development for Educators. (2008). *A prescription for success: What every educator needs to know about Response to Intervention and differentiated instruction.* Peterborough, NH: Staff Development for Educators.

Strothman, S. (Ed.) (2001). *Promoting academic success for students with learning disabilities: A Landmark College guide.* Putney, VT: Landmark College.

Taymans, J. M., West, L. L., & Sullivan, M. (Eds.). (2000). *Unlocking potential: College and other choices for people with LD and AD/HD.* Bethesda, MD: Woodbine House.

Tilly, W. D. Response to intervention: An overview. (2006, Winter/Spring). *Special Edge, 19*(2), 1–10. (Online newsletter.) Retrieved from http://www.calstat.org/textAlt/SpEDge_eng/win06edge.html#top

U.S. Department of Education. (July 2000). *My child's special needs: A guide to the individualized education program.* Retrieved from U.S. Department of Education Web site: http://www.ed.gov/parents/needs/speced/iepguide/index.html#closer

Vogel, S. (2005). *College students with LD: A handbook.* Pittsburgh, PA: Learning Disabilities Association of America.

Web Sites

- All About Adolescent Literacy
  http://www.adlit.org/
- Council for Exceptional Children
  www.cec.sped.org
- Dyslexia at College: Information for Dyslexic Students at College or University
  http://www.dyslexia-college.com
- Families and Advocates Partnership for Education (FAPE): Helping Parents and Advocates Improve Educational Results for Children with Disabilities
  www.fape.org
- Landmark College Institute for Research and Training
  http://www.landmark.edu/institute/index.html
- Monahan and Cohen
  www.monahan-cohen.com
- National Association of State Directors of Special Education
  www.nasdse.org
- National Center for Learning Disabilities RtI Action Network
  http://www.rtinetwork.org
- National Center on Response to Intervention
  www.rti4success.org
- National Dissemination Center for Children with Disabilities
  www.nichcy.org
- National Research Center on Learning Disabilities (numerous articles and information on RtI)
  www.nrcld.org

- Parent Advocacy Coalition for Educational Rights (PACER Center)

  www.pacer.org
- Reed Martin

  www.reedmartin.com
- Strategic Instruction Model

  http://reach.ucf.edu/~CENTRAL/secondary/SIM/index.html
- Technical Assistance Alliance for Parent Centers

  www.taalliance.org
- U.S. Department of Education (information on IDEA 2004)

  http://idea.ed.gov
- U.S. Department of Education, Office of Special Education Programs' IDEA Web site

  http://idea.ed.gov/explore/home
- Wrightslaw

  www.wrightslaw.com
- Wrightslaw Yellow Pages for Kids

  www.yellowpagesforkids.com

Index

for, 282; and parents, 183, 184–185, 288
Individuals with Disabilities Education Act (IDEA): history of, 282; on rights of special education students, 182, 282–283; and RtI, 274, 277–279, 284–285; on specific learning disabilities, 3, 5–6; and testing accommodations, 244
Infants, risk factors for dyslexia in, 11
Instructional methods: for composition, 133-139; for comprehension, 106–114, 261–262; for decoding, 73–76, 79–84; for differentiating instruction, 232–236; for fluency, 19, 92–96; key elements of, for students with dyslexia, 45–49; National Reading Panel recommendations on, 19; for phonics, 68–70; for phonological awareness, 18–19, 63–65; for prewriting, 129–131; for revising and editing written work, 140–145; for spelling, 118–125; for vocabulary, 98–103, 260–261. See also Activities; Games; Response to Intervention (RtI)
Intelligence: of people with dyslexia, 7; and processing speed of brain, 22–23; reassuring children with dyslexia about, 179. See also Gifted students

Intelligence tests, 31
International Dyslexia Association, dyslexia definition of, 4
Intervention: importance of early, 8, 18; research-based, for struggling readers, 35–42, 172–173. See Response to Intervention (RtI)
Irregular words, 87, 89

J

Junior high school students: reinforcing reading skills of, at home, 203–205; symptoms of dyslexia in, 14–15

K

Kress, J., 90

L

Language skills: difficulties with, 12; games and activities for strengthening, 159–162
Learning disabilities (LD): defined, 3, 5; evaluations for, 28–29; organizations that address, 294–297; parents' talking with child about, 178–181; specific, 3, 5–6, 27
Learning styles, 47–48, 194, 213, 232
Legal advocates, 186
Local education agency (LEA), 282, 285, 286
Long-term projects: parental help with, 197, 212; teacher's help with, 228, 229, 251, 293
Loynachan, C., 125, 163

M

Mapping: mind, 131; semantic, 113, 261; story, 114, 256; word, 102, 122–123

Mariconda, B., 135

Mason, L. H., 138

Math: adaptations of materials for, 239; difficulties with, 13, 14, 15; memory problems in, 20, 21; mnemonic technique for, 254; writing accommodations for, 156, 157

Meetings: IEP, 288, 289; tips for parents on, 184–185

Memory difficulties: examples of, 20–21; as reason for comprehension problems, 105; testing for, 32; tips for teachers to help students with, 253–257. *See also* Mnemonic techniques

Metacognition: and brain function, 22; general information, 48, 104, 106, 107; strategies for learning, 107–108, 174. *See also* Self-monitoring

Middle school students with dyslexia: reinforcing reading skills of, at home, 203–205; symptoms in, 14–15

Miscue analysis, 76–78

Mnemonic techniques: to aid comprehension, 112–113; to help with memory difficulties, 253–255; for revising and editing, 144–145; for steps in composition, 138–139; for study skills, 214–215

Modifications: general information, 224–225; homework, 227; of learning materials, 237–239; when to use, 225

Motivation, tips on increasing, 198–199, 230–231

Motor skill difficulties, 11–12, 23

Murray, B., 122–123

Music, 255

N

National Center for Learning Disabilities (NCLD), learning disability definition of, 5

National Institute of Child Health and Development, 16

National Reading Panel, 19, 96

No Child Left Behind Act, 50

Nolan, S. M., 144

Note taking, 215–216

O

Online resources. *See* Web sites

Oral language, tests of, 33–34

Oral reading: as accommodation, 154–155; to build fluency, 92–94; of draft when revising compositions, 141; guided, 19; parents' encouragement of, 202. *See also* Fluency

Organization: parental help with, 206–209; teacher's help with, 246–249

Organizations, national. *See* Web sites

Orton, S., 35

Orton-Gillingham (O-G) method: reading programs

How to Reach and Teach All Children in the Inclusive Classroom

Practical Strategies, Lessons, and Activities, *2nd Edition*

By: **Sandra F. Rief, M.A.** and **Julie A. Heimburge**

ISBN 978-0-7879-8154-9
Paperback | 480 pp.

This thoroughly updated edition gives all classroom teachers, special educators, and administrators an arsenal of adaptable and ready-to-use strategies, lessons, and activities. It is a comprehensive resource that helps teachers reach students with varied learning styles, ability levels, skills, and behaviors. The authors offer a team approach that includes parents, colleagues, and learning specialists, enabling teachers to guide diverse groups of students in grades 3–8 toward academic, social, and emotional success.

How to Reach and Teach All Children Through Balanced Literacy

User-Friendly Strategies, Tools, Activities, and Ready-to-Use Materials

By: **Sandra F. Rief, M.A.** and **Julie A. Heimburge**

ISBN 978-0-7879-8805-0
Paperback | 352 pp.

The balanced literacy method combines the best practices of phonics and other skill-based language instruction with the holistic, literature-based approach in order to help you teach reading, writing, and speaking in a clear and approachable format. The book includes detailed descriptions of what a balanced literacy classroom looks like and shows how to create a program from the ground up or give your existing program a boost. This reference can be used across content areas and is filled with reproducible worksheets, activities, and other handy classroom tools.